"*But God the guider of all good actions . . . did drive them   by his providence*

ir desired port, beyond all their expectations; for never any of them had seen that coast."
—Captain John Smith

Cape Henry, Virginia, first landfall of the Jamestown
settlers in the New World, April 26, 1607.

"This Iseland . . . is low ground, full of Marches and Swomps, which ma.

aire, especially in the Sumer, insalubritious and unhelthy."—Bacon's and Ingram's Proceedings

Jamestown Island, near Black Point.

They found wild turkey "of an incredible Bigness, partridge, pigeons, deer, rat

They found wild turkey "of an incredible Bigness, partridge, pigeons, deer, rat

, *raccons, bear, panther, elk, wild cat, buffalo, possum, wild hog.*"—Robert Beverley

American puma, coastal South Carolina.

"What could they see but a hidious & desolate wilderness, full of wild beasts & wild men .

d ye whole countrie, full of woods & thickets, represented a wild & savage heiw."
—William Bradford

Cape Cod: Tom's Hill, fourth campsite
of the Pilgrim exploration party.

"... we came to our seating place ... where our shippes doe lie so neere the shoare that th[...]

The Birth

by John Lewis Stag[...]

A Ridge Press Book/Gross[...]

... moored to the Trees in six fathom water." —Master George Percy   Jamestown Island and the James River, Virginia.

# of America

xt by Dan Lacy

Dunlap, Publishers, New York

Editor-in-Chief: Jerry Mason
Editorial Director: Adolph Suehsdorf
Art Director: Albert Squillace
Managing Editor: Moira Duggan
Art Associate: David Namias
Art Production: Doris Mullane

The Birth of America, by John Lewis Stage, text by Dan Lacy.
Photographs and text protected in all countries
of the International Union for the Protection of Literary and
Artistic Works. All Rights Reserved, including the right
of reproduction in whole or in part. Prepared and
produced by The Ridge Press, Inc. Published in 1975 by
Grosset & Dunlap, Inc. Published simultaneously in Canada.
Library of Congress Catalog Card Number: 74-29439
ISBN: 0-448-11545-X
Printed and bound in Italy by Mondadori Editore, Verona.

Contents

Introduction

Reading Samuel Eliot Morison's *Oxford History of the American People* some ten years ago gave me my first and strongest sense of our colonial forefathers as people. I remember feeling, too, that there seemed to be historical inevitability at work in the long story of their evolving time and place, that the Revolution with which our colonial life ended was the logical capstone of an uniquely American experience.

In fact, of course, a rather rare thing had happened: A people had risen not only to throw off tyranny, but with the declared intention of establishing liberty and justice through government by consent of the governed. For that time, or any time since, these principles were lofty and enlightened, and, as colonial America was superseded, they enabled a new nation of united states to embark on an adventure in democracy that continues to this day.

For a photographer, Professor Morison's evocation of this history stimulates a thousand pictorial images, and in that ferment this book began.

Not immediately, to be sure. Years passed in which I went about my business, photographing on assignments from magazines the people and environments of foreign countries. Usually I prepared myself by reading the country's history; my pictures were not necessarily historical, but the national character as it appeared to me seemed always related to the formative influences of the past and the nature of the land.

Eventually, I felt a growing desire and obligation to pay my respect to my own heritage. The techniques that had served me well abroad proved equally applicable to my native land. I read, took notes, and tried to discover the surviving realities of colonial life in contemporary America. Much had vanished, but much exists, and that which does continues to have immediacy and point. When I see the sword of Myles Standish, it helps me to visualize the man and strengthens my belief in his existence. Similarly, Washington's field compass, Franklin's bifocals, and the mild Virginia tobacco that flourished in Jamestown colony's streets give me a handhold on the actuality of the past.

Over a period of several years I lived among landmarks of colonial America, in every case photographing as faithfully as could my vision of both the reality and significance of the past.

The photography that resulted and is preserved in this book is quite within the range of my own style; I was on a self-assigned mission after all, and acting as my own editor, and I seized every opportunity to put into effect pictorial ideas that I might not have attempted for a lesser venture. Pictures were taken in all seasons—in the cold of a Cape Cod winter and the heat of a Charleston summer. They were taken under all the conditions—sunlight, moonlight, candlelight—I thought it likely the colonial settlers had experienced.

I was surprised and delighted by the cooperation of museum directors, local historical societies, and curators of collections in permitting the precious items in their care to be removed from their cases and photographed in actual historical settings. Picture samples from one place smoothed my way at the next, until finally it was unusual to encounter a turn-down anywhere. I was allowed into privileged places early, late, and off-season. I placed my historical "props" without protest. I hope I made it clear how grateful I was.

The text was written after the photographic sequence was established. I have appreciated the opportunity to collaborate with Dan Lacy, and been pleased by the consonance of our two modes of history.

—*John Lewis Stage*

Acknowledgements

Behind the sometimes formidable names of historical organizations are people.
Of the hundreds who have helped with the photography for this book there are a number who
have given so much of their time, support, and enthusiasm that I would like to
express my appreciation publicly. They are: Thomas W. Whitford, Jane Carson, Lawrence Couter,
Lawrence Geller, Joann Doll, Shirley Bischoff, Jacqueline Taylor,
Frank Hammond, Barrington Clary, Jody Doyle, Susan Finlay, Ann Hawkes Hutton, John Hetzel,
Vincent Kehoe, Jane Pape, John Lauth, Jean May, Nancy Mohr, Louise Stackdale,
Bill Richards, Hugh De Samper, Dwight Storke, Larry Whipple, David Little, and Nancy Campbell.
Special thanks are due to Betsy Foster, my assistant, and to my wife, Gillian Stage,
who contributed unstintingly of her unique sense of her adopted country.

1. The First Settlers

Only a few miles separate Jamestown and Yorktown, where English rule began and ended in what is now the United States. Too often in our minds these sites seem to lie as close in time as they do in distance. Pocahontas and Betsy Ross, Myles Standish and Paul Revere mingle as though they were near contemporaries in our school-day recollections of American history.

But the facts are otherwise. Between the two Virginia landmarks lie one hundred and seventy-four years. Between Yorktown and the present lie nearly two centuries more. The American Revolution is at the midpoint, not the beginning of our history. George Washington's inauguration lies closer in time to Richard Nixon's than to the landing at Jamestown. From Sir Walter Raleigh's "lost colony" on Roanoke Island to the drafting of the Constitution is a longer span than from the Constitutional Convention to our own day. The colonial period we think of as an early infancy in fact embraces half our national existence.

And it was in that long genesis that the shape of American life was fixed. The ideas proclaimed in the Declaration of Independence were not new ones. They reflected views of men and government in which Americans had long believed. The notion that all men are created equal is at least as old as Christianity and the Roman Stoics, but it was on the colonial frontier that it gained reality for Americans. Freedom was natural to men who for nearly two centuries had ruled themselves an ocean away from kings and bishops and dukes and standing armies.

The abounding American faith in the future was a staple of the colonial temperament and the natural bond of a people united not by their varying pasts but by their common future. Restless movement was a pattern set by generations of men and women who crossed the Atlantic, followed the rivers of the new continent into the back country, pressed against the mountains, and flowed through the passes they found into the valley of the Mississippi. Ceaseless change, evolving newness are the oldest and most fixed elements in the American tradition.

The elaborate structures of European society were lost in the transatlantic voyage. The colonists brought the common law, but not the higher English courts or the panoply of solicitors and barristers. They brought a knowledge of arms, but no standing armies; a knowledge of crafts, but no guilds; Christian faith, but not bishops or cathedrals. In particular, the dying load of feudalism was left at home. Pragmatism—testing ideas by how they work—dominated colonial life as it does our own today.

The worst aspects of American life as well as the best were formed in the colonial period. It was then that Americans began to think of the continent as an inexhaustible reservoir of raw materials and resources that could be heedlessly used up and relentlessly despoiled. Racism grew side by side with liberalism, and conscience did not stop the white men from slaughtering Indians and driving them from their land, or from buying black slaves to work the endless acres of the New World.

For good or ill, most of what we are now we became then; and one who would understand the America of the twentieth and twenty-first centuries would do well to ponder the America of the seventeenth and eighteenth.

Time rushes over this changing land. Hundred-story buildings rise over the foundations of the Dutch huts of New Amsterdam and six-lane expressways obliterate the footpaths of the colonists. But there remain beaches and mountains and meadows that are as they were when the first explorers saw them. Buildings great and small have survived the centuries and the bulldozers. Restorations—at Jamestown, Plymouth, Philadelphia, Williamsburg, and elsewhere—have stayed time and preserved the architecture, furnishings, and artifacts of a place and era.

Museums display tools, clothes, weapons and household effects. The sensitive eye can still look back through time and see the life of our forefathers and the land where they lived it. And across those centuries we see, as in an ancient mirror, our very selves as we were in the morning of our history.

II

When English settlers first came to America it was not to an unknown world. More than a century lay between Columbus's landfall at San Salvador and the first permanent English settlement at Jamestown. During that century the Spaniards created an empire in Mexico, Peru, and the Caribbean. French canoes voyaged the chill rivers of the north. Spanish horsemen rode the Arizona deserts.

Even the coast from Maine to Georgia had been skirted by hundreds of European ships. Italian seamen other than Columbus sailed in the service of nations bordering the Atlantic. The naturalized Venetian Giovanni Caboto, or John Cabot, explored the North Atlantic coast for Henry VII of England while Columbus was still making his later voyages to the Caribbean. A Florentine, Giovanni da Verrazano, flew the French flag in his voyage from the Carolinas to Maine in 1534. Spanish treasure ships from the Caribbean lumbered up the coast from Florida to the Chesapeake or beyond, borne by the Gulf Stream and sometimes pursued by Drake, Hawkins, and other English freebooters. Countless fishing vessels, seeking cod off Newfoundland and Labrador, were blown south along the New England shores.

Accounts and rumors of the new land had poured into England for a century. As the strength of Elizabethan England grew, merchants and noblemen hungry for money and glory looked more and more eagerly west across the sea. At first they reached tentatively, with little expeditions financed by a single nobleman—a Raleigh or a Gilbert. But after Spain's great Armada was destroyed in 1588, and English merchants grew wealthy enough to form trading companies and finance expeditions, the movement west became a steady and unending stream.

The first Europeans to come to America were not seeking to rebuild in a new world the life they knew at home. They sought the unique riches of an untapped hemisphere which would compensate them for Europe's lacks—mountains full of gold, silver, and jewels, tropical lands that could grow the sugar and spices and dyewoods killed by Europe's frost, and northern forests where warm furs could be found for the robes of the wealthy. And these they discovered. Spain took the gold and silver of Mexico and Peru, the logwood and dyes of Central America, the sugar of the Caribbean. The French found furs.

For the later English settlers there was left only the temperate zone between—land reminiscent of England, with good stands of oak, ash, and pine, and fertile fields where English wheat, barley, and peas would grow. The summers were hot, but not too hot for Englishmen to labor; the winters cold, but not too cold to be endured. It was a land that would welcome them, where English farms and families and towns could rise, and a new England be made.

The first Englishmen to see this America were eager explorers, men who burned with the desire to rival Spain and build an English empire beyond the sea. They viewed it with eyes that had been made ready to see a paradise. Wherever they looked they saw what their eagerness wanted to see.

In 1584 Arthur Barlowe and Philip Amadas were sent by Sir Walter Raleigh to find a site for a colony. Raleigh planned a base along the South Atlantic coast from which English ships could prey on Spanish treasure fleets. Amadas and Barlowe made a landfall on the Outer Banks of North Carolina and took possession of the land in the name of Queen Elizabeth. When they came to Roanoke Island, in the sound behind the Outer Banks, the explorers saw Indian gardens growing, and planted English peas to test the soil. Barlowe found it "the most plenti-

Opening pages: Contemporary re-creation of "James Towne, Land of Virginia," which lost more than half its colonists by the end of the first summer, survived a "starving time" in 1609–10 and a bloody Indian massacre in 1622 to become, finally, the first permanent English settlement in the New World.

ful, sweet, fruitful, and wholesome of all the world."

It is little wonder that Barlowe's report led Raleigh to seek to secure Roanoke Island. In 1585 six hundred men commanded by another of Britain's many great sailors, Sir Richard Grenville, set out in seven ships. Some three hundred intended to be settlers, but there were no women among them. Roanoke was to be a military post, not a colony.

Grenville returned to England in September, leaving Ralph Lane in command. Lane actively explored the mainland as far north as Chesapeake Bay. But he antagonized the Indians by his brutality, and by spring, when Grenville was expected to return, he was openly at war with them. The colony was short of food and supplies. It hungered desperately in wait of the supply ship. Weeks passed, and when Francis Drake appeared by chance with his fleet of freebooters Lane's colonists abandoned Fort Raleigh to sail home with him. Among them were Thomas Hariot, an acute scientist and observer, and John White, a gifted artist. Hariot's *A Briefe and True Report*, published in 1588, and White's drawings, widely circulated as engravings, were produced as propaganda to encourage the Crown to support Raleigh's colony, settlers to come there, and wealthy men to invest in it. But they were truthful within their limits and give us the best picture we have of the Atlantic coast before English settlement.

Hardly were Drake's ships beyond the horizon when Grenville's relief expedition appeared. Finding the post abandoned, Sir Richard contented himself with leaving a handful of men to hold the island for another year.

In the spring of 1587 came a true colony—men, women, and children with seed and tools and household goods. They were the first English men and women who crossed the sea not to explore but to remain, to give up England and become Americans. They were led by John White, the painter of the 1585 expedition. They had intended to stop by Roa-noke Island only to pick up Grenville's men and then go on to the Chesapeake Bay area to settle. But all they found was a ruined fort and a moldering skeleton. An impatient sea captain, anxious to be away from the dangerous North Carolina coast before the season of storms, left them on the island ånd sailed back to England. White returned with him to get more supplies, but not before his daughter Eleanor, who was among the colonists, bore a baby girl, Virginia Dare, the first English child born in America.

The fate of this group is unknown too. The threat to England of the Spanish Armada made a relief expedition impossible in 1588, and it was not until 1590 that White came again to Roanoke. Once more only the vestiges of an abandoned colony were found, with the fresh-cut letters CROATOAN on a tree to hint at their destination. Probably the colony, despairing of White's return and driven by hunger, had moved to Croatan, a village of friendly Indians near an inlet in the Outer Banks. Here they may have hoped to live on oysters and fish. Storms kept White from going over to Croatan, and decades passed before Englishmen came again to Roanoke. No trace of the settlement remained. It had become the legendary "lost colony."

III

The first two English ventures to survive, the mother sites of America, were at Jamestown, on the James River in Virginia, and at Plymouth, on the shores of Massachusetts Bay. Both were business ventures financed by the London and West Country businessmen who had replaced such venturesome gentry as Sir Walter Raleigh in the promotion of English colonization. Both survived agonizing years to demonstrate the feasibility of American settlement; both saw their importance dwindle and nearly disappear as other settlements came to dominate their regions.

Jamestown was a project of the Virginia Company. Late in 1606 the company dispatched one hundred and forty-four colonists in two small ships, the *Susan Constant* and the *Godspeed*, and a tiny pinnace, the *Discovery*. Their voyage was difficult. Contrary winds held them off the English coast for weeks, and they then had a storm-battered crossing to the West Indies. Arriving in March, they rested and sunned and bathed for three weeks among the islands of the Caribbean, taking on fresh food and water. More storms were encountered as they sailed up the Gulf Stream to Virginia. In April the ships finally entered Chesapeake Bay. For days the colonists lived aboard ship, making brief expeditions ashore, and exploring upstream in search of a permanent site.

It was full spring in Virginia, and the land seemed a heaven to the sea-weary eyes of the settlers. "There we landed and discovered a little way, but we could find nothing worth the speaking of but fair meadows and goodly tall trees, with such fresh waters running through the woods as I was almost ravished at the first sight thereof," wrote the young nobleman, George Percy.

The enchanted view of the land changed quickly enough. In English eyes the smiling children of nature who welcomed them with food and dancing became ruthless savages. The warm and healing climate and pleasant glades became steaming marshes and breeders of pestilence. In the midst of abundance, starvation wrenched the bellies of settlers too lazy or improvident to hunt and fish or plant and tend crops. The actuality of the first settlement at Jamestown became a hell.

As the site of their colony they finally selected a peninsula jutting into the James River, about sixty miles from the ocean. Sometimes they called it James Fort, sometimes James Citie, in honor of the king; but its name has survived as Jamestown. In May the colonists landed and English occupation of America began.

Jamestown had much to recommend it. It was far enough from the sea to be hidden from Spanish ships and to receive warning of an invading fleet. The main channel of the river swept close to the shore, so that ocean-going ships could be moored to trees along the bank.

But the leaders of the colony ignored the instructions of the Virginia Company to pick a high and healthy site. More than half the peninsula was marsh, filled with mosquitoes, and fatal to the unacclimated settler. For a decade most of those who came to Jamestown died in their first year.

The settlers built a little triangular fort on a site now washed away by the river, a bit more than half a mile downstream from the brick church tower which is the only surviving remnant of seventeenth-century Jamestown. Within the fort were a church, a storehouse, and the colonists' huts.

The early settlers were a poor lot to open a new land. Half were gentry who held themselves above all labor. Most of the rest were employees of the Virginia Company with virtually no stake in the colony and little skill for the tasks before them. Few were farmers or builders or woodsmen. In fear of an Indian ambush, they cowered in the palisaded fort, bickered endlessly among themselves, and were obsessed with the dream of finding gold.

Had John Smith not taken charge, they would have starved in their fecklessness. Many indeed did. George Percy wrote that "Our men were destroyed with cruel diseases, as swellings, fluxes, burning fever, and by wars; some departed suddenly; but for the most part, they died of mere famine." More than half of them died in that first summer.

John Smith was a twenty-seven-year-old soldier, a farmer's son, used to a rough life. In the midst of incompetents he soon became the true leader of the colony, and in the summer of 1608 he was made its legal head as president of the Council. He befriended the Indians, got corn and game from them, and ruthlessly held the colony together. A major new expedition meanwhile set out from England in May, 1609. Nine ships bore five hundred colonists, including women and children. The expedition was headed by Sir Thomas Gates, who had been one of Drake's lieutenants in the relief of Roanoke Island, and whose powers as governor of Jamestown were to be absolute. A storm split the fleet, however, and Gates's ship, *Sea Venture*, along with one other, was blown off course and wrecked on Bermuda. The hundreds of new settlers in the remaining seven ships arrived, leaderless, in August.

Smith, who had been badly burned in a gunpowder accident, departed on one of the returning vessels. He left a colony that seemed firmly established, a colony of nearly five hundred settlers provided with arms, tools, clothing, and livestock. But hardly had he sailed when things began to go to pieces again. The Indians, who had been quieted by Smith's diplomacy, resumed their earlier hostility. They killed dozens of the colonists. Farming was abandoned. Discipline disappeared. Starving men ate dogs, rats, and even the bodies of the dead. Houses and palisades were torn down for firewood. By May, 1610, hardly sixty persons were left alive. At that time Gates arrived with the survivors of the Bermuda wreck, but they too were desperate and without food.

No course seemed possible but to abandon the colony and seek food among the fishing fleets off Newfoundland. The settlers boarded ship and sailed in June, 1610, ready to leave Jamestown another failure. Almost miraculously, before they had reached the mouth of the James, they met still another expedition from England, commanded by Lord De la Warr.

De la Warr had three hundred men and supplies adequate for a time. The starving settlers returned and re-entered the broken village, but their troubles were not ended. Disease and hunger still riddled them, and half the remaining colonists died over the winter of 1610–11. De la Warr himself became so ill he had to return to England, leaving the colony under the rule of the iron-willed deputy who had come with him, Thomas Dale. He and Gates, both of them harsh men, were governors for the next five years. They brought the colony the peace and discipline it needed, and at last growth was steady.

The turning point may have come in 1612, when John Rolfe managed to get seeds of the mild South American tobacco so popular in Europe and plant them in Jamestown. By 1614 he had grown a crop large enough to send to England, where it was sold at very high prices. Immediately Rolfe's strain displaced the bitter and unsalable native tobacco, and every field in Virginia seemed to promise a fortune. Men became as mad for tobacco as they had been for gold. Corn was abandoned, defenses were forgotten. Even Jamestown's streets were planted to the weed.

The Virgina Company now ceased its effort to profit by hired laborers and sought to gain from quitrents on the land itself. Fifty acres were offered every person who came to Virginia at his own expense, or paid the passage of another. Efforts were made to encourage other settlements, and by 1619 both sides of the James were sprinkled with farms and plantations as far inland as the falls that mark the present site of Richmond. Attracted by cheap and abundant land on which to grow a highly profitable crop, settlers began to pour across the ocean. The colony was made even more attractive in 1619 by the creation of an assembly through which the settlers could make their own laws. This was the first legislative body in America.

In 1622, peaceful coexistence with the Indians, which had persisted since the uprising after Smith's departure, was shattered by a surprise attack in which nearly four hundred settlers were massacred. Violent weather and a plague among the cattle nearly finished the colony off. In view of these difficulties, the Virginia Company did not oppose termination of its rights in Virginia. The Crown took over the colony and stability was restored.

Fifty years of relative peace and prosperity permitted the rapid growth of Virginia. Farms and tobacco plantations filled the James Valley to Richmond and spread to the banks of the York and the Rappahannock. The open waterways, bringing ships to every planter's dock, made it unnecessary to develop a port city like New York or Boston. Hence, Jamestown itself grew but slowly. The little dry land on the marshy peninsula was soon taken up. A governor's residence was built, as well as a series of statehouses and churches. In 1676 Jamestown was still a village, but a proud one, and the seat of government for a rapidly growing commonwealth.

In that year Indian warfare broke out all along the frontier from New England to Virginia as expanding settlements pressed against tribesmen desperate to hold their dwindling lands. Frightened farmers in the westernmost settlements of Virginia slashed at nearby Indians and demanded that the government at Jamestown raise an army to protect them. William Berkeley, the aging and autocratic governor, refused. The frontiersmen then formed their own army and chose as their leader a dashing, scapegrace young aristocrat, Nathaniel Bacon. Bacon was still in his twenties, newly come to Virginia for the greater peace of his wealthy family in England. He moved forcefully against the Indians, friendly tribes as well as hostile, and slaughtered them mercilessly.

He and his followers then turned their attention to Jamestown and the governor. Among the small farmers of the West there was a smoldering hatred against the arbitrary rule of Berkeley and his handful of wealthy cronies. There were dramatic confrontations in the streets of Jamestown: the old governor tearing open his coat and daring the young rebel to shoot, while cowering burgesses peeked from the statehouse windows. For months the two antagonists maneuvered treacherously against each other, until finally Berkeley fled and Bacon's men burned to the ground almost every house in the hated capital.

Bacon had triumphed, but he died suddenly of fever, not yet thirty, and his army melted away. Berkeley returned to the ashes of Jamestown. A new statehouse was erected and the village half-heartedly rebuilt, but the glory of Jamestown was over. A few years more and the capital was moved to Williamsburg, then known as Middle Plantation. After 1700 Jamestown was only a county seat, drifting quietly into obscurity, a forgotten foothold upon the great continent, where English men and women survived hunger, fever, and arrows to begin the building of America.

IV

Plymouth, like Jamestown, was a merchant venture, but with a vast difference. While most of the early settlers of Jamestown were adventure-seeking young gentry and footless laborers, the core of the Plymouth settlers was an earnest and disciplined band of Pilgrims. They were simple men and women seized with a naked sense of God's immediate presence. Their convictions carried them beyond the Puritans, who were willing to remain in the established church they sought to purify, and led them into separate congregations in which only the winnowed and accepted few could join together. Persecuted in England, a band of these separatists took refuge in Holland. But fearing that their children would be absorbed into the worldly society of that hospitable country—then reveling in the creature comforts of its lucrative world-wide mercantile enterprises—they sought a more distant refuge in the American wilderness. They engaged a merchant company to finance the voyage and promised to repay from the produce of the joint labor of the settlers. The separatists were probably never a majority of the Plymouth Colony, but they ruled it. And their discipline never permitted the disorder and chaos that nearly destroyed Jamestown.

The Pilgrims set forth in two crowded ships, the *Mayflower* and the *Speedwell*. The latter proved unseaworthy and the expedition had to turn back and load everyone onto the already overcrowded *Mayflower*. They were long delayed and finally reached Cape Cod in November, 1620, far north of their planned destination on the Hudson. New England winter was already closing in. For two weeks they explored the semicircle of Cape Cod Bay in a little shallop, despite an Indian attack and stormy weather that nearly wrecked their tiny craft. Driven ashore, exhausted, in what they were to call Plymouth Harbor, they abandoned their plans to reach the Hudson and decided to make a home here, in the midst of snow and bitter gales.

Plymouth did have some advantages. The harbor offered shelter for ships. A brook promised fresh water and there were abandoned cornfields about that would save the hard labor of clearing land for the first crops. (The Pilgrims were making themselves heirs to the labor of Indian tribes nearly wiped out by an epidemic, probably of smallpox, brought by earlier European fishing fleets.)

The men went willingly and vigorously to work, beginning on Christmas Day, 1620. A street was cleared, running along the northern bank of the brook from the beach to a sharply rising hill on which a fortification of sorts was quickly built. A common house was rushed to completion and each family was charged with building its individual hut. Like the early houses at Jamestown, and like Indian dwellings, these had walls of "wattle and daub" and thatched roofs. It took all winter to finish construction while the *Mayflower* lay impatiently at anchor to provide housing. Not until March, 1621, were all ashore.

As soon as possible the Pilgrims replaced their early huts with more substantial houses. These were built on heavy timber frames with brick or stone foundations. Walls were of hand-hewn clapboards, or sometimes of vertical planking.

The houses were small—most of them having a single ground-floor room of three to four hundred square feet, with an enormous fireplace and chimney. In this room the family lived, worked, cooked, ate, and slept. A partition might afford some privacy for the parents' bedroom and a partially floored loft might supply sleeping space for children.

Plymouth houses were well built, but never grand or luxurious. Simplicity, solidity—the elements of Pilgrim character—were their virtues.

This same simplicity appeared inside the houses. The great fireplace was the center of family life. From it swung hooks and rods on which pots could be hung. A simple table served for dining, and also for sewing, reading, and writing. Benches provided most seating, though better homes had one or more chairs of simple but clean design. There were surprising numbers of tablecloths and napkins. Tableware might be wooden plates with metal spoons for soups and liquids. The more prosperous had earthenware or perhaps pewter dishes (though hardly china) and steel knives. By the 1700s a few of the wealthy may have had some silverware and even forks.

Chests served as closets and bureaus. Great and small, they were used to store clothing, work materials, foodstuffs, tableware—whatever the family had to keep. Bedsteads were large, with cords in lieu of springs. Each bedstead was covered with a mattress stuffed with rags or feathers.

Clothing, too, though more colorful than one might expect, was simple and durable. Over a linen shift a Pilgrim woman wore a petticoat or underskirt, with a heavy skirt to the ankles, and a chemise and bodice. Heavy shoes and stockings provided protection and warmth. Sinful hair was concealed beneath a cap. Dress was sober, but women took obvious pride in a "best" outfit of softer material with decorative ruffs.

Men wore heavy breeches cut like full knickers and fastened below the knee, with a short jacket or doublet and a cloak coming to the knees. Boots and heavy stockings might be covered with canvas leggings. The tall hat of Pilgrim tradition was for Sundays. A cap or bare head did for work days.

The history of Plymouth is quieter

than that of Jamestown. The simple dignity of the Pilgrim faith made for sobriety and earnest work. No golden crop like tobacco tempted its settlers. Livelihoods were gained by hard work on rocky farms and in weather-beaten fishing boats. Though many prospered, none became really wealthy as wealth was measured in the larger colonies. The religious bonds of the congregation and the requirements of the mutual welfare made Plymouth Colony a far more closely knit body than Virginia. Individual Virginians spread across a whole commonwealth to clear and manage their own plantations; Jamestown was only the governmental nucleus of this sprawling domain. Plymouth Colony grew as well, but only as groups received permission from the mother congregation to depart and found a new town and church. New settlements remained under the control of the General Court at Plymouth.

The Pilgrims were less greedy than their neighbors in dealing with the Indians and for most of the colony's life lived at wary peace with them. The great exception was King Philip's War in 1675–76. Many individual incidents combined to precipitate this conflict. But its fundamental cause was the steady expansion of the New England colonies, and especially of Plymouth, into the lands of the Wampanoags, a tribe that had always been friendly. Their able young king, called Philip by the whites, was provoked beyond endurance in the summer of 1675 and led a coalition of tribes in an effort to exterminate the English colonies, or at the least to check their spread into Indian land. For months Philip was brilliantly successful, wreaking a great slaughter on the whites. But finally the combined strength of the New England colonies and the Indians of other tribes who joined them was able to harass Philip's scattered troops into starvation and desertion. In 1676 Philip himself was surrounded and killed. His head was impaled on the little fort at Plymouth and his whitening skull hung there for decades.

Though Plymouth had achieved steady growth and quiet prosperity, it was overshadowed from its early days by the Massachusetts Bay Colony to the north. Wealth, learning, and military power were there, and close connections with important Puritan noblemen and merchants in Oliver Cromwell's England. The growth of Massachusetts Bay was much more rapid. It quickly overcame Plymouth's ten-year head start and far surpassed it in population. More important still, Massachusetts enjoyed the protection of a royal charter under the Great Seal of England, while Plymouth existed only by royal tolerance. Efforts to persuade the Crown to give Plymouth the protection of a similar charter failed.

Finally, all charters were abrogated by James II, who in 1686 set up a single Dominion of New England, embracing not only Massachusetts, Plymouth, Rhode Island, and Connecticut, but also New York and New Jersey. The Dominion was to be ruled by a royal governor without an elected assembly. Plymouth, like the other colonies, was compelled to yield. But Edmund Andros, the governor of the Dominion, had hardly begun his reign when James II was dethroned by the Glorious Revolution.

All the colonies now entered a scramble for new charters, each seeking the maximum power and territory for itself. Plymouth was too small to advance its claims vigorously. Sanctimoniously declaring an intention to protect Plymouth from being swallowed up elsewhere, Increase Mather, the energetic representative of Massachusetts Bay, won a new charter in 1691 that merged Plymouth into the larger commonwealth. The Old Colony was at an end. Thereafter Plymouth, like Jamestown, survived only as a county seat, no longer a colonial capital.

It left, however, a rich body of legend: the first Thanksgiving, the Pilgrim Fathers, John and Priscilla Alden, the valiant Myles Standish, the saintly William Bradford, and a tradition of simple goodness that has sweetened our history.

"We landed all our men, which were set to worke about the fortification, others some to watch and ward as it was convenient." Thus the first landing at Jamestown as described by settler George Percy in his journal. *Right: Tiny English merchant ships* Susan Constant, Godspeed, *and* Discovery *debarked 104 men and boys after eighteen-week Atlantic crossing. Below: Arms in Jamestown guardhouse. Indians attacked settlers twelve days after their landing.*

". . . the marketplace and streets and all other spare places planted with tobacco . . . the Colonie dispersed all about, planting Tobacco," Captain John Smith noted in 1617. Mild Virginia leaf (l) was a great success in Europe and crucial source of income for Jamestown colony. Left & above right: Houses were of wattle-and-daub construction. Roofs were reed thatch, periodically replaced.
Above left: Kiln for pottery made from riverbank clay. Settlers, mindful of distance from England, strove for self-sufficiency in housewares.

*Pilgrims landed in winter storms of 1620 with
determination to establish a godly home in the wilderness.
". . . they now had no friends to welcome them nor inns
to refresh their weatherbeaten bodies," wrote New Plymouth's
Governor William Bradford. Right: "Plimoth Plantation"
re-creation is based on records of 1627. Below: Shallop
transported Pilgrims between ship and shore.
Detail of* Mayflower *restoration. Plymouth rock.*

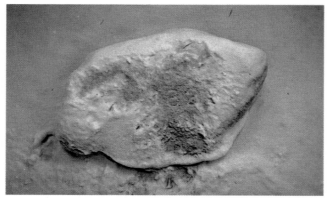

Right: Helmets, halberds, pikes, and matchlock muskets in Plimoth Plantation home of Captain Myles Standish. Top: Corn, furs, and tools in Common House which also served as trading post. Left: Standish's rapier, swords of John Carver and Elder Brewster. Above: Standish's razor.

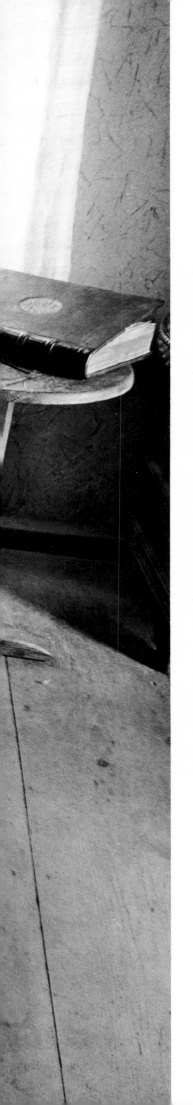

Opposite: Cradle brought on Mayflower *rocked new-born Peregrine White. Chair and Bible were Governor Bradford's. Above: Pilgrim clothes were as bright as native dyes could make them. Stockade sheltered settlers' gardens. In background is flat-topped fort and meeting house. Surgical instruments (l) in home of Samuel Fuller, Plymouth physician. Most illnesses were treated with herbs or by bloodletting for relief of disturbed "humors" and "tempers."*

Preceding pages: "I make no question," Edward Winslow wrote back to England from Plymouth in 1621, "but men might live as contented here as in any part of the world." Above: "Indian corn, even the coarsest, maketh as pleasant meat as rice." Right: The First Thanksgiving. "Our harvest gotten in, our Governor sent four men on fowling, so that we might after a more special manner rejoice together, after we had gathered the fruit of our labors. . . . At which time, amongst other recreations, we exercised our arms, many of the Indians coming amongst us . . . whom for three days we entertained and feasted."

2.
New
England

New England was born of the marriage of the Puritan faith to a rugged and winter-blasted land. Not all New Englanders were Puritans, and of those who were few managed to realize in their daily lives the ideals of their faith. Yet Puritanism left its imprint on every aspect of the life of colonial New England. So did a formidable geography. The hills and fields had been heavily scoured by the glaciers of the last ice age, and only a thin layer of stony topsoil covered its granite skeleton. The sea had eaten away the northern coastline; there was no level tidewater plain—only the waves pounding against the rocky edge of the hill country. Only in Rhode Island and parts of Connecticut were there stretches of fertile and level land.

Freezing weather came early, lasted long, and bit deeply. Cattle had to be housed and fed through the winter and enormous quantities of firewood had to be cut and split by ax. Travel was difficult when the roads were frozen and impossible through the seas of mud left by spring thaws. No river leading into the interior was navigable by seagoing vessels, so that waterborne commerce was slight. Farm products were difficult to get out, foreign imports difficult to get in.

These conditions added greatly to the burden of daily labor. To maintain a self-sufficient family farm in Massachusetts men and women simply had to work harder than in Pennsylvania or Virginia. The growing season was shorter, the yield scantier, the fields were more difficult to clear and plow, the crops harder to get to market, and more energy had to be spent in building stout housing. The land itself echoed the Puritan lesson that life was real and earnest, and that only the sober and diligent could survive it. Though New Englanders had a lusty affection for life, they could not afford frivolity and waste.

The fact that their farms yielded nothing for export comparable to the flour of Pennsylvania or the golden tobacco of the South meant that New Englanders had to find other means of paying for imported necessities, and for this they turned to the sea. New England-built ships sailed all the oceans and made up a large part of the merchant marine of the colonies and of England itself. New England merchant captains traded in the ports of Europe, West Africa, and the Caribbean—wherever British ships could enter. Codfish plucked from the cold Atlantic as far north as Newfoundland became the principal source of New England wealth, while the distilling of rum from molasses was the key industry in a self-renewing pattern of trade. New England ships delivering fish and Pennsylvania flour to the West Indies returned with sugar and molasses, then took rum to Africa to barter for slaves, who were delivered for sale to the southern colonies or the West Indies.

The great men of New England were no lordly planters presiding over rural estates, like the Lees and Randolphs of Virginia or the Van Cortlandts or Van Rensselaers of New York. They were townsmen and merchants, like the Derbys of Salem, the Hancocks of Boston, or the Browns of Providence. Their great houses, with elegantly carved doorways and magnificently furnished rooms, were town houses, not plantation manors like Mount Vernon or Westover. Cities like Boston and towns like Exeter, Salem, Providence, and New Haven played a role in New England very different from that of Virginian villages.

While trade drew New Englanders out to the Atlantic world, religion turned them inward and marked the special nature of New England life. A majority of migrants to the region were Puritans and all of them were English. There were almost none of the Irish, Scottish, German, French, and African strains that varied and enriched the colonies to the south, nor was there a continuing stream of settlers from England itself to keep alive a sense of identity with the homeland. The peak migration to the region came in the early decades of the seventeenth century, when tensions between king and commons were leading England toward civil war, and Puritans were suffering under the Crown's hostility. After 1642, when strife between Cavalier and Roundhead began, immigration into New England ceased almost entirely. By the late 1700s most New Englanders could look back to at least three generations in the New World—to more than a century in which their inbred Puritan identity had been fixed. John Winthrop had called the Massachusetts Bay settlement "a city upon a hill" as an example to all mankind of a society that conformed to God's will. The sense of being a chosen group charged with a special mission permeated New England thinking.

Along with the sense of separateness went a sense of community within New England. The churches which played so central a part in New England life were not parishes, as in the Catholic and Anglican faiths, but congregations. A church was not a division of some central body established to serve a defined geographic area; it was rather a freely associated body of men and women who were not individually affiliated to some abstract "church," but who themselves *were* the church, self-governing and subject to no priest or distant bishop. The importance of centralized town and village life, as contrasted with the dispersed agricultural society of the South, heightened the sense of community. Towns and congregations often were nearly identical, the town meeting and the congregational meeting comprising the same united group of men governing themselves in matters civil and religious.

For all these reasons, the maritime, fishing, trading New Englanders, the most far-traveled of all the colonists, remained also the most provincial, the most firmly rooted in their own way of life.

By no means were all New Englanders Puritan Congregationalists. The unchurched were a large part of the population there as elsewhere.

Nor were all Puritans alike. On the side of the orthodox there was the Mather-Cotton dynasty. John Cotton and Richard Mather were English Puritan ministers, leaders of the faith, devout Calvinists, learned scholars, who came to Massachusetts with the early settlers. Mather married John Cotton's widow after the death of his own wife, and his son, Increase Mather, married Cotton's daughter, who in turn bore him a son, Cotton Mather. For three generations these men rooted themselves at the center of the Puritan regime in Massachusetts. They were full of zeal in the pulpit and active in the civil affairs of the colony. Increase Mather was president of Harvard. Cotton Mather, though driven with fear of devils and witches, was yet a leader in scientific thought and a bold early advocate of vaccination against smallpox. Books poured from their pens, written in awe of what they thought to be the visible daily presence of God in the affairs of Massachusetts.

For Cotton and the Mathers and like-minded men, government was the church's instrument for erecting a framework of godliness, and it should allow nothing to threaten the true faith. Any man and woman who saw God and one's duty to Him through different eyes clearly had to be made to conform or be driven out. Thus, when Roger Williams and Anne Hutchinson came, each in one way or another challenging the rightness of orthodoxy, the answer of the Puritan establishment, led by Cotton, was to cast them out. Williams had to make his way, alone and on foot, through driving storms of snow and sleet until he reached the shore of Narragansett Bay, where he could buy land and establish a little settlement of his own. Anne Hutchinson, a heretic more remote from orthodoxy even than Williams, and a female challenger of male dominance to boot, was driven out later with her little band and followed Williams's lead to the free land of Rhode Island.

The half-starving Indians who rose in anguish as expanding white settlement ousted them from their cornfields and hunting grounds appeared to

Opening pages: Topping Tavern, at Shaftsbury, Vermont, was a haven on the Glastonbury stage road for travelers who endured the winter snow, spring mud, and year-round ruts of sparsely settled rural New England. A tavern, church, and school were required by law in most communities.

the Mathers and their followers not as desperate fellow humans but as fiends from Hell sent upon them in punishment for the colony's lapses from orthodoxy. The Puritan leadership spurred on the Puritan soldiers and rejoiced when the tribes were slaughtered.

Though he was anxious lest the innocent be wrongly charged, and urged caution in seeking out the Devil's accomplices, Cotton Mather was one of those who saw witchcraft at work in the colony and drew sober and painful satisfaction from the cleansing fire in which convicted witches were burned at Salem in 1691–92. The stern arm of the law, made pitiless by the love of a jealous God, must keep pure the ways of God's commonwealth in Massachusetts.

Roger Williams, although banished into the New England winter, was as much a Puritan as Cotton or the Mathers. As a London boy of little means he had somehow caught the eye of Edward Coke, the lion of the common law in Elizabeth's reign, the Attorney General and later Lord Chief Justice of England. Coke made the tall blue-eyed lad his clerk, saw to his education, and helped him into Cambridge and the ministry. Williams became a God-possessed man and came early to the Puritan refuge in Massachusetts. Here he preached to the landowners that their titles were void, since the land was the Indians' and could be lawfully owned only by purchase from them. He preached to the magistrates that their power was not from God and that the law dare touch no man's conscience. He wondered, in his innocence, that they rose and cast him out. But he stayed firm in his view even when he became himself a ruler in his own colony of Rhode Island. The province became a refuge for Quakers and Baptists driven from Massachusetts and Connecticut, who relied on Williams's declaration: "We have no law among us whereby to punish any for only declaring by words their mind and understandings concerning the things and ways of God, as to salvation and an eternal condition." In his own writing, as in *The Bloudy Tenent of Persecution*,

Williams made clear that the freedom he believed in was not just for other Protestants, but for Catholics, Jews, Moslems, and even atheists. His heart went out indeed to the pagan Indians, whose language he learned and whose friendship he won.

Yet Williams and Cotton and the Mathers fully shared the Puritan conviction that to find and adhere to the true faith was life's one important goal. Cotton and the Mathers thought it so important that the state must be called on to trample out error. Williams thought it so important that an erring state must never touch religious faith.

To the Puritan conscience it was not possible for a man to throw the burden of his salvation on the church, accepting its guidance with blind faith. Each man had to make his own judgment of God's will, with the Bible as the ultimate source of guidance. It was essential that men and women be able to read for themselves the Scriptures and the sermons and devotional works of their religious leaders.

The preeminent role of commerce in New England life added a secular need for reading, writing, and arithmetic. Hence, education was valued in New England as nowhere else in the colonies. Village schools for teaching elementary subjects were required by law. The publicly supported Boston Latin School was founded in the early days of the colony and still exists. Other schools prepared students for college, while Harvard (1636), Yale (1702), and Rhode Island (1765), later renamed Brown, prepared them for the ministry or for law.

Like all the seventeenth- and eighteenth-century world, New Englanders were very conscious of social rank. Early legislation forbade common folk to dress with the elegance of the upper classes. Youth bowed to elders, the unlettered to the educated, all men to the ministers and elders of the church. Workmen in the ropewalks and sail lofts of Boston pulled their forelocks when a Hancock passed in his coach and four. The graduating class at

Harvard was listed in the commencement program not in alphabetical order, or the order of their grades, but in the order of the social standing of their fathers.

But for all this, New England society was the most democratic the civilized world then knew. Church membership was confined to that minority whose sober lives and professed faith were thought to deserve it, but the church was governed by the votes of its members in their individual congregations, not by a hierarchy. The ballot was confined to landowners, but in New England this included the majority of adult men. And the affairs of each town were not delegated to important officials as matters too profound for the common, but were debated and voted on in open town meetings.

The people ruled, not only in the towns and congregations, but in the colonial governments. In seventeenth-century Massachusetts, and in Rhode Island and Connecticut throughout their history, the governor was the people's man, chosen by their representatives, and councilmen, judges, and sheriffs—like town selectmen and congregational ministers—were the people's servants.

Though the Puritan faith might view all men as base and worthless creatures beneath God's angry gaze, yet it held them equal in their worthlessness, each separately and immediately answerable to God, each important to God as one of His own souls. To be a farmer, even a very small farmer, or a householder in a village in New England was to be one's own man, standing sturdily and independently with the mighty in the eyes of the law and of God.

The energetic, determined, zealous society that grew up along the New England coast spread rapidly throughout the Northeast. Massachusetts men and women moved westward to the beautiful Connecticut Valley, settling in Windsor and Northampton and Deerfield. Remote from the bustling commerce and growing worldliness of Boston, the simpler life of early Massachusetts was renewed in these frontier farms and villages.

The cranky "come outers" who could find no spiritual home elsewhere took refuge in Rhode Island's freedom, slowly building a colony on the shores and islands of Narragansett Bay, whose superb harbors in time would draw them into a sea commerce as brisk as Boston's. Rhode Island slavers, whalers, and traders would be known around the world.

Conservative Puritans, who found the mother colony of Massachusetts too lax rather than too rigid, moved to New Haven on Long Island Sound and started anew the effort to build and preserve a sacred commonwealth. They founded Yale College as a bulwark of orthodoxy, safe from the growing heresies of Harvard.

To the north a few hardy Massachusetts families sought the fisheries of Maine, and the tiny royal colony of New Hampshire was founded at the mouth of the Merrimac River. The kingly white pines of the northern forests, stretching unmarred toward the sky, provided perfect masts for the Royal Navy and a livelihood for Maine and New Hampshire woodsmen. By the late eighteenth century even the rocky, mountain-locked valleys of Vermont were attracting a few of the hardiest New Englanders. To the south, trading sloops passed from Connecticut across Long Island Sound, and the eastern end of the island became an extension of New England, with white-steepled churches facing village greens.

The vigor and intensity of New England life could not be contained in its mountain- and sea-girt corner of the land. In time its men and women would press westward, pouring across the Mohawk Valley of New York into the Western Reserve, the lands along the Ohio shore of Lake Erie, and eventually into all of middle America. And the ideas of New England were destined to travel even farther, so that almost every aspect of American life would be touched by its stubborn individualism and earnest commitment.

"The truths of God are the pillars of the World," declared Nathaniel Ward of the Massachusetts Bay Colony. The severe Puritan view of man's existence demanded that each individual look into his own soul, dedicate himself to God's grand design, and accept His holy word, the Bible, as the complete guide to life. The life style based on this direct and steadfast faith is reflected in the homes of the early Puritans. Left: Simple shingled façade of the Hoxie House, a 17th-century salt box at Sandwich, Massachusetts. Above & right: Casement windows and steep-pitched roof of Elder John Whipple's home, built in 1640, at Ipswich.

New England's unpainted wooden homes
were made small for easier
heating in winter. Interiors were
a clutter of homemade furniture, bedding,
tools, and drying vegetables and
herbs. Above: Smith's Castle at Wickford,
Rhode Island, where Roger Williams
preached. Left: Parson Capen House built by
Topsfield, Massachusetts, congregation
for its new minister in 1683. Right:
Hoxie House kitchen, sleeping
loft, and children's play furniture.

Left: Plymouth's Town Brook turns wheel at John Jenney's grist mill, which appears as it did in 1636, when it ground Pilgrim corn. New England's fast-moving streams also powered early industry, such as iron works at Saugus, Massachusetts, which was founded in 1647 to convert local bog ore into nails, tools, and other sorely needed colonial hardware. Below: Ironmaster's House. Bottom: Items preserved at Works' reconstructed forge.

Witchcraft: ". . . on the 19 of January in the morning he swooned, and coming to himself he roared terribly and did eat ashes, sticks, rug yarn." So wrote Increase Mather of a case of purported possession by the Devil. Satan was as real as God in New England and the earthly battle for men's souls never-ending. Witches were Satan's envoys, and when superstitious religious fear gripped Massachusetts in the 1690s, some 200 persons were accused of being in league with them. Twenty were executed. Gallows Hill (opposite) at Salem was a scene of hangings during mania. Above center: Burial plot and home of Rebecca Nurse, who was hanged despite testimony of friends and neighbors. Left: Her chair. Above: House of Seven Gables at Salem (l) and reproduction of pillory (r) at Newburyport.

Above: Three bulwarks of society—the school (foreground), tavern, and church—on village green at York, Maine. Right: York's First Parish Congregational Church (1747) reflected in window of Emerson-Wilcox House. Above right: Trinity, a classic Anglican church in religiously tolerant Newport, Rhode Island. Opposite: Interior of Trinity, with books sent from Church of England in missionary effort to support the Anglican faith.

New England believed in education and civic responsibility. Harvard College was established in 1636. Hebrew text and notebook on sill of window overlooking Massachusetts Hall (l) belonged to Jonathan Trumbull, Class of 1727, later colonial governor of Connecticut and ardent patriot during Revolution. Top: Hingham, Massachusetts, meeting house also served as church.
Above: Lottery ticket signed by John Hancock helped finance Boston's Faneuil Hall. School at York, Maine (r & above r). Education for all was mandatory in Massachusetts Bay Colony as early as 1647.

Beautiful, hand-carved, broken-pediment doorways marked growing stability and prosperity of Connecticut River Valley in 1700s. Farms of Essex, Wethersfield, Windsor, and Deerfield were fertile, and river was only navigable one in New England. Salt-box houses were simple, balanced, economical— like their occupants— but highly stylized doorways were expressive of a degree of comfort entering rural life. (Pediment is "broken" by gap in sweeping curves atop door frame.)

Codfishing and triangular maritime trade route between New England, the West Indies, and Africa brought wealth to Salem, Boston, and Newport. Opposite: Salem residence and office of Elias Hasket Derby, first American to die a millionaire. "King Derby" built family fortune by underwriting profitable privateering ventures during Revolution. Right: Tools of Samuel McIntire, a talented carpenter-architect who built Peirce-Nichols House (above) owned by East India merchant prince Jerathmiel Peirce. Above right: Rocky New England coast at Kittery, Maine.

*The Look of Winter: After 150 years of settlement,
New England, though still subject to the English king,
felt itself American and had evolved a new breed
of independent, self-reliant Yankees. Above: Farmstead
at Coventry, Connecticut. Opposite, from top:
Weathercock in southern Vermont, horse and sleigh in western
Massachusetts, and White Horse Tavern in Rhode Island.*

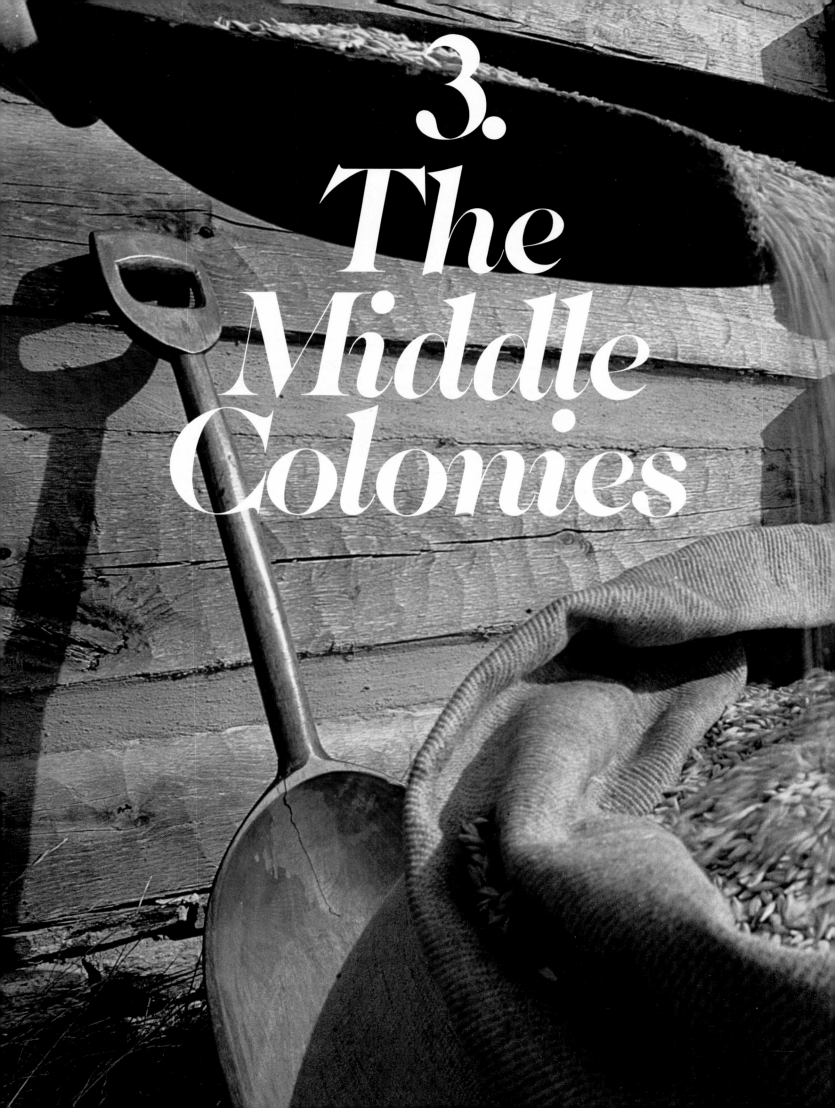

3.
The Middle Colonies

While a compact society, homogeneous in its English descent and Puritan faith, was being created in New England, the middle colonies—New York, New Jersey, Pennsylvania, and Delaware —were becoming the prototypes of the American melting pot.

New York had been New Amsterdam until 1664, settled by Dutch farmers and merchants and French-speaking Walloons from what is now Belgium. In the communities along the Hudson River from New York to Albany, Dutch was a common language throughout the colonial period. Dutch families—Van Rensselaers, Van Cortlandts, Stuyvesants, Philipses, Bergens, Schuylers—dominated the province as near-feudal landowners.

The first settlements along the Delaware River were of Swedes and Finns, and their influence persisted, especially that of the Swedes, in the colony of Delaware. Pennsylvania was a proprietary colony, granted to William Penn, the Quaker leader, in recognition of the services to the Crown of his father, Admiral Sir William Penn. He intended this rich domain as a haven for his fellow Quakers, and to protect their religious liberties he extended a like liberty to all. Quakers were the predominant sect—in power and wealth if not in numbers—in Philadelphia and the surrounding counties. But the fertility of Pennsylvania's limestone soils, the accessibility of Philadelphia as a port, and above all the personal and religious freedom the colony offered, made it more attractive than any other to the following waves of immigration. Most particularly it appealed to thousands of German peasant families who found their painful way to America in the eighteenth century when wars, agricultural changes, and religious oppression dislodged them from their homeland. Many of them were Calvinists or Lutherans, but thousands more were Mennonites or Moravians who shared the pacifist convictions of the Quakers. Coming to Pennsylvania, they settled beyond the Quakers, in the area around Lancaster and York. Over large parts of the colony the German language prevailed in churches, newspapers, businesses, and offices of local government.

After the Germans came Scots from northern Ireland. They settled along the rugged frontier in the pinched valleys of the Alleghenies.

In New Jersey, the western area along the Delaware was Quaker in religion and tied to Philadelphia socially and commercially. The eastern half looked to New York and shared that city's ethnic and religious diversity, though with a strong Scotch-Irish strain. New York also acquired a substantial number of the hundreds of thousands of Huguenots who fled France to escape the energetic persecutions of Catholic Louis XIV.

No single faith placed its stamp on the middle colonies as Puritanism did on New England. There were two separate established churches in New York—the Dutch Reformed and the Anglican—and in Pennsylvania there was none. The idea of a secular state, in which every man was free to follow the faith he chose and the government concerned itself with none, was born of American religious diversity and had its beginning in Pennsylvania.

Like New England, the middle colonies had little to send Britain directly to pay for their imports. England had no need for their wheat or flour, so the New Yorkers and Pennsylvanians were forced to sell in other markets. But they were luckier than New England in the abundance that poured from their fertile fields. Wheat grew easily, and bumper crops were turned into flour in hundreds of mills scattered along the region's rivers. Rich pasture supported fine herds of horses and cattle. Dense hardwood forests provided the staves for barrels and hogsheads. Horses, cattle, salt beef and pork, flour, lumber, casks, and barrels were exported from New York and Philadelphia to the Madeira and Canary islands and to the Caribbean in exchange for wine, sugar, molasses, and money.

Financing the commerce of the colonies presented special problems. There were no banks in America and little hard money. The colonies were forbidden to issue coins and in any case had no sources of gold and silver. The few British half-crowns and gold sovereigns that found their way across the Atlantic were soon drawn back to pay customs duties, quitrents, and the bills of British merchants. The coins that actually circulated in the colonies were largely foreign—Dutch florins and Spanish milled dollars, the legendary "pieces of eight." Indeed, the Spanish coin was the forebear of the American dollar. "Two bits" as a slang term for a quarter refers to two "bits," or eighths, of the piece of eight, which was stamped so it could be broken into eight parts.

The colonies developed substitutes for hard money. Barter was prevalent and in the southern provinces tobacco was legal tender for paying debts, wages, and taxes. Warehouse receipts took the place of actual tobacco and became a form of currency. Colonial legislatures often voted an issue of paper money, but it had a low and variable value and was worth little or nothing outside the colony that issued it. Royal vetoes of colonial legislation authorizing paper currency further limited its use. Perhaps the most useful substitute was the system of bills of exchange. These were drafts issued by colonial planters or shippers against the merchants to whom they had consigned shipments of tobacco, rice, or other products.

If a planter waited for his annual tobacco crop to reach a London merchant and its value to be shipped to him in sterling, he would be without payment for months. Instead, he issued a draft on the merchant for all or part of the estimated value of the shipment, and used it to pay his local bills. Eventually the draft, or bill of exchange, came to someone who owed money in England. He would send it to the London creditor, who collected from the merchant on whom it was originally drawn. The bills were an awkward form of money, dependent for their value on the reputation and solvency of both the issuer and the merchant on whom drawn, but they were indispensable, given the restrictions on colonial finance.

The trade of the middle colonies with the Caribbean Islands thus had a special significance. The rich sugar planters of the tropical islands shipped far more to Europe than they imported. As a result they had strong boxes filled with gold and silver coins and sound bills of exchange that could be used to pay for shipments imported from New York and Philadelphia. The merchants of those cities therefore had ready cash beyond the resources of any other port or colony, and they played the roles of bankers and insurers as well as merchants. With this advantage, and with the rich farmlands about them as a base of operations, they soon passed their rivals in Boston in wealth and in the volume of their commerce.

Seagoing ships from England, the Mediterranean, and the Caribbean came and went on the tides—through the Narrows and across New York Bay, or past the Capes and up the Delaware River. At the same docks, merchants' sloops were loaded with cargoes for the coastal trade—ironware and cloth, fine china and silver, tea, sugar, tobacco and books that had come from England and the colonies to the south. To the little ports along the Hudson and Delaware rivers and on Long Island Sound they brought the long-awaited imports, and refilled their holds with flour and lumber and salt meat destined for the merchants' warehouses and shipment abroad.

By the late eighteenth century Philadelphia was one of the world's important cities, the largest in America and second only to London in the British Empire. It was the first large city to be built on the grid pattern of modern American cities, with equidistant streets crossing at right angles. William Penn had planned it, including the reservation of squares as city parks and the intersection of the thor-

Opening pages: The middle colonies—from New York to Delaware—were America's granary. Fertile fields, industrious immigrant farmers, energetic Quaker merchants, and Philadelphia's port all encouraged bountiful productivity. From Lancaster area in 1750s came the Conestoga wagon which later took pioneers west.

oughfares of Market and Broad streets, the widest in the world, at the city's center. The plain but well-designed brick houses that, row on row, filled downtown Philadelphia showed both the substantial wealth and the Quaker simplicity of the city.

Philadelphia was Benjamin Franklin's town. He had come as a youth of seventeen in 1723, when the city was just entering the period of its greatest growth. Franklin throve there as he never could have in the structured life of his native Boston, or in the rural existence of Virginia or Maryland. Franklin was born for the fluid, changing life of a city in which society was arranging itself in new patterns, without the bonds of an established church or a fixed social order—where the test of any institution was not whether it conformed to tradition, but whether it worked.

Franklin organized a hospital and a library, an insurance company, a learned society, and a university, while also becoming the city's leading publisher and one of its wealthier men, a consummate diplomat and political leader, and one of the century's greatest scientists—all in one lifetime.

Franklin was profoundly respected in the colonies, even beloved, but never fully understood. Other American thinkers drew their ideas from tradition: conservatives from the great body of English law which Blackstone's recently published *Commentaries* so brilliantly summarized, and from the dogmas of the church; liberals from Locke and Harrington and the Puritan writers of the seventeenth century. Franklin often spoke and wrote almost as though he had never read these thinkers of the past but was seeing all society anew with eyes undimmed by inherited concepts. He moved easily to the common-sense solution of every problem, usually finding it in the voluntary cooperation of like-minded men.

Far more than any other eighteenth-century man, Franklin foreshadowed what American life was to be. Jefferson's words and Washington's deeds are honored and remembered, but both of them were shaping antique concepts to a new continent's needs. Our actual lives are lived in the light of Franklin's mind: pragmatic, experimental, optimistic, future-looking, bearing little baggage of the past. No city in the world of his time was more filled with the future than the Philadelphia of Benjamin Franklin.

New York was a smaller and less advanced Philadelphia. Most of the farmlands of New York were still held in feudal estates descended from patroonships, the vast domains granted by the earlier Dutch government. One family, the Philipses, owned most of what is now Westchester County and much of the Bronx, ruling it from their Yonkers manor house and doing their trading and grinding of wheat at the Upper Mills in Tarrytown. Comparably vast estates lined the Hudson to Albany. These were farmed by tenants rather than by slaves or indentured servants, but it was hard to get men to spend their days working and improving other men's holdings. The way to freer land in the west was barred in New York by the rugged hills of the Highlands and the Catskills, and the powerful Iroquois athwart the Mohawk Valley.

As a result, few settlers came to New York. They passed to the more abundant and fertile lands and freer laws of Pennsylvania and the colonies of the South. New York remained one of the smaller colonies, and its hinterland could not support so large a city as Philadelphia. Nevertheless, the city of New York was able to achieve substantial growth. It filled the lower end of Manhattan Island and surpassed Boston in population, becoming the colonies' second city. It was even more cosmopolitan than Philadelphia. Dutch, Germans, Huguenots, Negroes, Sephardic Jews, Scots, and Englishmen spoke varied languages on its streets. There were not even the gentle patterns of the Quaker faith to give uniformity or dignity to its manners or to slow its pace. Then as now, New York was the intense city, bubbling with life, seething with faction, living intimately with the world-ranging sea as no other port. It was the kind of city in which a poor and illegitimate West Indian youth like Alexander Hamilton could in a handful of years attend college, become aide to a commander-in-chief, marry a beautiful heiress from one of the great families, and in early manhood become a shaper of a nation.

New England and the South each developed a distinct pattern of life, drawn from powerful traditions implanted in and then altered by the American environment. The threads of these two patterns were to weave and interweave in American life through the later centuries. The middle colonies were too diverse a mingling to form and impress such a special character on the new land. Rather they were open to what the new land itself required. Experimenter, pragmatist, businessman—free of ideology, reaching out in every direction, joining easily in new ventures, unbounded by traditional acres or traditional dogmas—the new American was shaped not in Boston or the rural New England meeting house or the plantations of Virginia, but in the city streets of New York and Philadelphia.

But a shadow hung over these richest and happiest of the colonies. The mountains pressed close upon them, and beyond the mountains were the Iroquois, and beyond the Iroquois were the French. The Great Lakes along which the canoes of the French priests and soldiers and voyageurs moved west skirted New York and Pennsylvania. In western Pennsylvania, the junction of the Monongahela and Allegheny rivers formed the Ohio, the strategic point that commanded the gateway to the west. In northern Pennsylvania and central and western New York were the Five, later Six, Nations of the Iroquois Confederation. By the mid-eighteenth century, they were the only eastern Indian force that was still warlike, powerful, and independent.

This was the theater in which the contest for the West, indeed for the continent, would take place. Since the early 1700s, the New England colonies and most of the South had been free of serious and immediate Indian threat. But in the middle colonies the time of war and blood was yet to come.

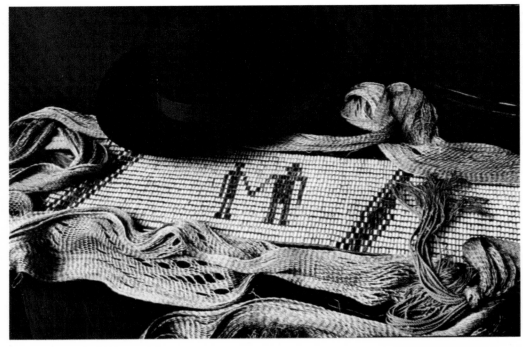

World of William Penn: "I intend to order all things in such manner that we may all live in love and peace with one another, which I hope the Great God will incline both me and you to do." So wrote the pacific Penn, expressing the brotherly philosophy he hoped would be the governing principle of his new colony. Opposite: Old Merion Meeting House at Ardmore, near Philadelphia, where Penn attended Quaker meetings. Top: Penn's wampum belt was a token of friendship from Indians. Sash, woven by Penn's wife, who remained in England, was worn on treaty-making occasions. Weathervane from 1699 mill at Chester bears initials of Penn and two partners who owned it. Right: Reproduction of Pennsbury Manor, on the Delaware River, where Penn lived for two years.

*Philadelphia—serene, dignified,
Quaker neat and prosperous, brimming
with culture—became the
largest city in America and second city of
the Empire. Laid out in orderly checkerboard design
by Thomas Holme, Penn's surveyor, it embraced
green parks and spacious avenues leading
to a center square for "the public buildings."
Clockwise, from left above: Medallion of
George II on Christ Church (1754), three views of
Delancey Street, Samuel Powel House
(1765), and Second Street Market (1745).*

Poor Richard

BEING AN

ALMANAC

EPHEMERIS

...tions of the SUN and MOON
...es and Aspects of the PLANETS;
THE
SETTING of the SUN;
AND THE
Setting and Southing of the Moon,
FOR THE

LORD 1...

Second after Leap... 54:

Preceding pages: Elfreth's Alley contained modest homes of working people. Young Ben Franklin's Junto, "a club for mutual improvement," met at No. 128. Left: Model of Franklin's bifocals—one of his many inventions—on title page of a 1754 edition of his popular Poor Richard's Almanack. *Clockwise, below: Hand press from his brother's Boston shop where he learned the printing trade. Franklin stove, another innovation. Franklin's traveling chess set, his book on electrical experiments, and an account of two balloon trips on which he sent the first air mail. Franklin's homemade generator.*

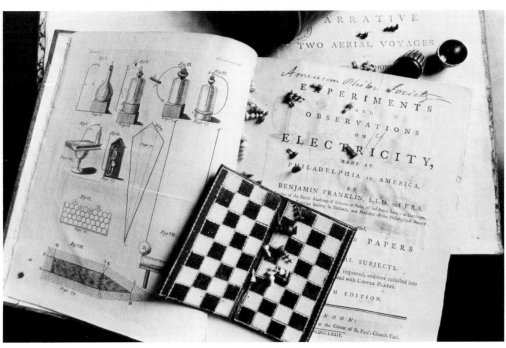

". . . any government is free to the people under it
(whatever be the forme) where the laws rule," wrote William
Penn as a guiding principle for a self-governing society
based on equality, reason, and tolerance. Early
structures of government in the middle colonies: Supreme
Court (above) in Pennsylvania State House (now known as
Independence Hall); court's dock for prisoners (opposite,
top). Bottom: The Court House, Delaware's capitol at New Castle.

Hudson River Valley was settled early
by the Dutch, whose substantial way of life
can be seen in limestone house of Jan
Van Deusen (opposite) at Hurley, New York,
and in Upper Mills trading post of
Philipsburg Manor at North Tarrytown
(below), which once controlled 90,000 acres.
Early Van Cortlandt portrait reflected
in mirror (far l) and Dutch cottage
interior (l) are at Van Cortlandt Manor
House, another formerly vast holding (80,000
acres) at Croton-on-Hudson, New York.
Bottles for gin and other spirits are
in dining room at Philipsburg Manor.

Utilitarian design of grist mill at Philipsburg Manor (l), precise fit of logs in Moon-Williamson House at Fallsington, Pennsylvania (r), and solid proportions of Old Swedes Church in Philadelphia (below) —with its traditional cherubim— reflect the thorough craftsmanship of the diverse groups drawn to the middle colonies. Dissimilarity of nationality and religion did not prevent settlers from sharing a commitment to the new land.

The West, promising open land and an independent
life, attracted immigrants who were pouring into
the colonies. The easiest route was through Philadelphia,
west on the Great Road past the fieldstone barns of
German farmers (r), themselves pioneers a generation
before, to the forest fringe, where a man could build
himself a log house like that at Daniel Boone
Homestead (l). Wadding for his fine Pennsylvania rifle
could be fashioned from nest of paper wasp.

4.
The
South

From the days of John Rolfe, when tobacco plants grew in the very streets of Jamestown, the golden weed dominated the life of the Chesapeake Bay colonies. The great wall of the mountains, close to the sea in the northern colonies, swung sharply west as it entered Maryland, leaving a belt of lowland and piedmont that widened from about a hundred miles to two hundred and fifty miles from the ocean to the Blue Ridge. In Maryland and Virginia, the eastern half of this area—the tidewater—was deeply penetrated by Chesapeake Bay, by great rivers—the Potomac, the Rappahannock, the York, the James—and by an interlacing network of creeks and inlets. Smaller ocean-going ships could come to the private docks of riverside plantations, and no man's farm, even the smallest, was far from navigable water.

This easy access to the Atlantic trade and to England encouraged a commercial agriculture based on exports, rather than the subsistence farming necessary in the back country. Virginians and Marylanders grew enough corn and kept enough hogs and cattle to feed themselves, but they depended on imports for most of their other needs. To pay for all they bought from England they had tobacco as their one great resource. And during the seventeenth century it gave them a golden time. The demand for tobacco seemed endless, not only in England but on the Continent, as more and more thousands became addicted to its use. Its cultivation was forbidden by law in Great Britain and was impractical in most of Europe. Virginia tobacco was sought everywhere for its quality.

Though taxes, insurance, and the charges of shippers and merchants as tobacco changed hands meant that the Chesapeake planters got only a small fraction of the sums paid by avid smokers, and though overproduction at times cut prices sharply, tobacco growing remained an extremely profitable occupation, with cash returns per acre several times that yielded by any other crop. There were, however,

two drawbacks. Tobacco was a hungry plant, quickly eating out the meager fertility of the thin and sandy soils on which it grew best. A few years' yield and the fields were ready to be abandoned to the leaching, gully-washing rains, while the backbreaking labor of clearing new fields was resumed.

The second drawback was that tobacco was a laborious crop. The tiny seeds had to be started in a tenderly prepared seedbed. Later the nursling plants had to be moved by hand to a carefully cultivated field. Throughout the hot summer the growing crop had to be hoed and weeded, kept clean of tobacco worms, and each plant topped and suckered by hand, so that only the choice center leaves were left to grow. At summer's end the leaves were hand-picked, tied into bundles, and hung to dry and cure. Finally, the following year, the dried leaves were carefully dampened and prized into hogsheads for shipment to market. Meanwhile, every day that could be spared had to be spent cutting trees, pulling stumps, and preparing new fields. No one man could manage more than a few acres of tobacco and also grow the foodstuffs and care for the livestock needed to sustain his family.

And yet there was all the endless land waiting to be exploited. Anyone could get for the asking a "headright" of fifty acres for himself, for each member of his family, including children and infants, and for each servant he brought to America. Men of wealth and influence could get far more. By the late 1700s there were families with tens of thousands of acres. And yet the land was useless unless men could be found to work it.

It was impossible to hire labor, for who would spend his days raising another man's tobacco when he might grow his own? During the seventeenth century Maryland and Virginia planters sought an answer in white indentured servants. These were men and women who came to America bonded to work for four to seven years for minimal food, clothing, and shelter in order to pay the cost of their passage. Some came willingly to find their fortunes in the New World. Some were spirited away from the taverns and slums of London by men seeking to profit from selling their labor. Others were convicts given their choice of American labor or British prisons.

But in the long run white servants were not a good answer to the planters' problem. Freedom came soon, almost as soon as the London townsmen learned the work of a Virginia tobacco plantation. And if it did not come soon enough for the worker, the forest and the frontier were nearby. Once he vanished into them he was almost indistinguishable from the thousands of other footloose white men pushing westward.

After about 1680 the planters looked elsewhere for their labor, to black men and women brought in chains from Africa or the West Indies and enslaved for life. Here was a far more satisfactory investment. When a planter bought a black he bought not the several years of uncertain work he got from an indentured servant, but the perpetual labor of the slave, and—if a woman—of all her descendants, forever. There had been blacks in Virginia since at least 1619, probably first as indentured servants. For the ensuing sixty or seventy years they were few in number. But from 1680 onward the British slave trade worked with ruthless efficiency, and slaves poured into the southern colonies in an endless stream.

It was the availability of slave labor that fixed the plantation system onto the South. Black slaves cleared the fields and built the mansions, served the tables, cooked the meals and polished the silver, tended the lawns and gardens, and cultivated the tobacco whose sale made it all possible.

Not all slaves worked on great plantations. Ten thousands of them worked in smaller fields side by side with their owners. Indeed, most owners were small farmers who had one or two slaves, as a New England farmer might hire one or two helpers. But the political and social patterns of the South were shaped by the great estates and the few hundred families who owned them.

Once riveted on the southern colonies, slavery and the plantation system were hard to change. The area lost economic flexibility. A southern planter could not, like a New England merchant, withdraw his capital from a less profitable enterprise and invest it in a more rewarding one. His capital was in human slaves who could not readily be shifted to other undertakings. And when planters became heavily indebted to British merchant creditors, they borrowed more on the security of the following year's crop and hence were compelled to continue to grow tobacco—and cotton, as British mills began to demand raw fiber, and the invention of the cotton gin made mass production possible in America—in the face of overproduction and falling prices.

Life was good for successful planters. Their thousands of acres stretched back from broad tidewater rivers. Their handsome red brick mansions were reached along avenues of carefully planted trees. Furniture and silver imported from England gave elegance to high-ceilinged rooms. Planters dressed in imported finery, were wigged and powdered for social occasions like London gentlemen. They traveled in their own sloops by river or in carriages or coaches imported from England and drawn by matched teams of horses. Liveried slaves served their well-laid tables.

The great planters, however, did not live in elegant ease. "Even the oldest of the colonial families could hardly count three generations of opulence, and most of their wealth had been wrung from a stubborn environment by its immediate holders. The storied plantation mansions to which so much tradition attaches were then but freshly erected in the ostentation of new riches. The slaves that worked their acres were not the faithful retainers of a later legend, but African tribesmen often not more than a generation from their savage freedom. The acres themselves were likely to be raw red clay newly

Opening pages: Refined and spacious home of George Wythe at Williamsburg is a miniature of the southern plantation residence. Like other colonial leaders, Wythe was a man of parts: classical scholar, law professor, Virginia burgess, judge, and signer of the Declaration of Independence. Foreground: What 18th century called "philosophical apparatus."

hacked from the wilderness. Beyond the nearby Blue Ridge the marauding Indians were still a real and bloody threat. No security of long-settled rents sustained the planters as it did the landed gentry of England. Bankruptcy awaited any owner who relaxed his ceaseless energy or failed in his power to manage men and events. The planter elite were imperious and able men who possessed great power, but not inherited privilege."[1]

Unable to compete with unpaid slave labor, smaller farmers were forced from the tidewater of Virginia and Maryland into the piedmont, beyond the reach of navigable rivers. Here they farmed for themselves, much like small farmers elsewhere in the colonies, with corn and hogs as their staples, working the fields with perhaps the help of one or two slaves. Their few purchases were paid for with the produce of a few acres of tobacco, and they lived in the yeoman independence of all back-country America.

Somewhat different patterns arose in the Carolinas and Georgia. Tobacco did not grow well in coastal South Carolina, but its marshy lowlands were ideal for the cultivation of rice. Vast estates were built on profits from rice and, in the later colonial period, indigo. Both crops required extremely hard and unpleasant labor in malarial lowlands, which was carried on exclusively by black slaves. The plantation system developed in a more extreme and aristocratic form than in the tobacco colonies. Absentee ownership was common and the wealthier planters spent much of the year in stately houses in Charleston, enjoying only the weeks of pleasant weather in spring and autumn on their estates. Charleston itself, with a magnificent harbor from which rivers or coastal channels ran to the plantation areas, became the center of the colony's life to a greater degree than the capital of any other province. It differed as well from the northern capitals like Boston, New York, and Philadelphia, whose leading citizens were urban merchants, lawyers, and businessmen. Though Charleston too had

its wealthy merchants, the great families were planters who had transplanted their aristocratic rural, almost feudal, society to an urban setting.

Most of the first settlers of Charleston were sugar planters from Barbados, already accustomed to an imperious style of life. Many who followed were Huguenots, bringing with them a French taste in cuisine, dress, and furniture. Much of the city was destroyed in a disastrous fire in 1739, but it was rebuilt at the peak period of the planters' wealth, with beautiful houses that faced inward on cool gardens, away from the bustle of the streets.

The high social season of Charleston, beginning in December and lasting through the winter, was the most dazzling in America. Ball followed ball. Silken-clad couples sparkled in minuets and gavottes they had learned from French dancing masters. Charleston was the musical center of the colonies as well. The St. Cecilia Society was famous for its concerts, and private entertainments were graced with performances of violin, flute, and harpsichord. The city's professional theater was the most active in America. Its race tracks attracted large crowds. The wealth of South Carolina rice and indigo planters was more solid than that of the Chesapeake tobacco lords. Hard money supported their elegance and kept it burnished. Even the most sophisticated visitors from Boston and New York were impressed by the grace and charm of the city's life.

North Carolina and Georgia had hardly developed a plantation system in the colonial period. Barrier islands, narrow inlets, and shifting sandbars made it difficult for ocean-going ships to reach the inland waters of North Carolina, and commercial agriculture dependent on exports did not thrive. Nor were there many immigrants who came directly to North Carolina from Britain or Europe. Instead, North Carolina was settled largely by small farmers from Virginia who had lost out competing with the big planters for land and had drifted south across the

[1]Dan Lacy, *The Meaning of the American Revolution*, New York, New American Library, 1964, pp. 57–58.

border of its less settled neighbor.

This small-farm economy placed North Carolina among the poorest of the colonies, with the fewest pretensions to aristocracy or learning. Until 1749 there was no printing press in the entire colony. There was not even a settled capital, the assembly meeting in Edenton, New Bern, or Wilmington as it chose. But there were compensations. If there were fewer plantations, there were fewer slaves and fewer wealthy slaveowners to lord it over lesser men. The most democratic of the southern commonwealths and the most individualistic, North Carolina was to be the first colony to vote for independence and almost the last to yield that independence to the Federal Union created by the Constitution.

Georgia was settled as a frontier outpost only in 1732, and at the end of the colonial period was still a straggling collection of farms stretching up the Savannah River. Originally proposed as a philanthropic effort to provide opportunity and an uplifting environment for unfortunates languishing in debtor's prisons, it had an uncertain start and began to prosper only as slavery was permitted near the end of the colonial period. Quickly thereafter a plantation system flourished and Savannah began to develop as a port.

After 1750, a new wave of immigration began to change the character of the southern colonies. The Germans and Scotch-Irish who poured into Philadelphia overflowed Pennsylvania and moved south down the Great Valley. They settled the area of Fredericksburg, Maryland, filled the Shenandoah Valley, and debouched through the James River water gap and other openings of the Blue Ridge into the piedmont of the Carolinas and Georgia. The Germans brought their religious faith, their careful and fruitful agriculture, their solid barns, and their handicrafts. The Scotch-Irish, as in Pennsylvania, pressed against the western edge of settlement, clearing the forests and driving back the Indians.

In every southern colony there was tension between the new settlers and the old. In Virginia most of the Germans and the Scotch-Irish settled in the Shenandoah Valley, separated from the older areas by the Blue Ridge. In the Carolinas they gained a footing west of the arid strip of pine barrens that slowed the westward expansion of the coastal settlements. The newcomers were small farmers, living off their own fields and pastures rather than growing tobacco and rice for export. Few of them owned slaves. They were Presbyterian, Lutheran, German Calvinist, and Moravian rather than Anglican. They were hard-working and God-fearing, resentful of wealthier eastern settlers and their aristocratic ways, bitter about the taxes levied by assemblies in which they were inadequately represented.

One group of settlers in North Carolina was of special interest: the Moravians who settled Salem in 1749. They lived communally, diligently clearing the land and farming with German thoroughness, trading fairly with all, including the Indians, bringing a rich devotion to music to the frontier, and founding North Carolina's oldest college. For more than a century their detailed records were kept in German, and the gentleness and seriousness of their society still survives.

The South grew with its roots in human slavery and with aristocratic convictions more strongly developed than anywhere else in the colonies. And yet this society based on the harshest kind of human inequality also inspired a devotion to public service and democratic government that eventually formulated the ideals of the Revolution and guided the new nation. To the power and wealth of the planter class was joined a sense of responsibility and public duty that produced a George Mason, a Thomas Jefferson, a Richard Henry Lee, a James Madison, a George Washington. It was the slaveholder Jefferson whose words dedicated the new nation to the proposition that all men are created equal, and the slaveholder Washington who won the new land's freedom.

Great houses and gracious living of plantation
society were supported by cultivation of tobacco, rice, and
indigo, and always by the labor of black slaves from
Africa. Left: Field hands tend tobacco at
Wakefield, Westmoreland County,
Virginia, birthplace of George Washington.
Above: Avenue of oaks, planted by slaves before 1743,
leads to Boone Hall, a 17,000-acre cotton plantation north
of Charleston, South Carolina. In time, nearly 1,000
slaves were required to work it. Right:
Spanish moss frames colonnaded Hampton Plantation,
near Georgetown, South Carolina.

"Like one of the Patriarchs, I have my Flocks and my Herds, my Bond-men and Bond-women, and every Soart of Trade amongst my own Servants, so that I live in a kind of Independence on every one but Providence."—William Byrd of Westover. Manorial life Byrd described existed in a setting resembling English country estate. Landscaped gardens (l) of Middleton Place, in Charleston, are oldest in America. Below (l to r): Thomas Jefferson's Monticello, Byrd family's Westover, which overlooks James River in Virginia (and bears early eagle symbol on its gateposts), and George Mason's Gunston Hall, a neighbor to Washington's Mount Vernon. Pages 94-95: Stratford, home of the Lees of Virginia, in Westmoreland County. Although the use of brick was traditional in the South (as middle colonies used stone and New England wood), Stratford's style is an unusual survivor of heavy Jacobean taste.

*"When the candles were lighted, we all repaired . . .
into the dancing-room. First each danced a Minuet; then all
joined as before in the country dances." Gaiety,
glitter, and polished taste of Virginia's gallants and fair
women are recalled in this description of a visit to
Stratford (below l) in 1773, and exemplified in dried flower
bouquet (opposite) and carved woodwork of Palladian
drawing room (below) at Gunston Hall. A young English
wood-carver, William Buckland, was brought to Virginia to
complete the interiors in the latest London taste.*

"It is possible," wrote a Swiss traveler, marveling at American hospitality, in 1702, "to travel through the whole country without money, except when ferrying across a river." In the social code of southern society, hospitality was a point of honor, and the guest arriving at Wakefield with trunks (far l) would be welcomed, however long his stay. Visitors meant long evenings of good talk, as well as dancing and fox hunting. Planters, many of whom had been schooled in England, valued education, and most plantations had special schoolhouses like that at Stratford (l). Tutors (in effigy, above), especially Scots and divinity graduates, were hired for their no-nonsense approach in study of Latin and Greek classics.

Work of the Plantation: Overseer's office at Stratford (opposite) displays major crops— tobacco, cotton, flax, and corn. Top: Reproduction 17th-century ketch for Carolina-Georgia coastal trade. Deep, navigable rivers enabled boats to anchor at each plantation's wharf. Left & above: Three views at Wakefield—a span of working oxen, Potomac from master bedroom, air-curing of tobacco.

103

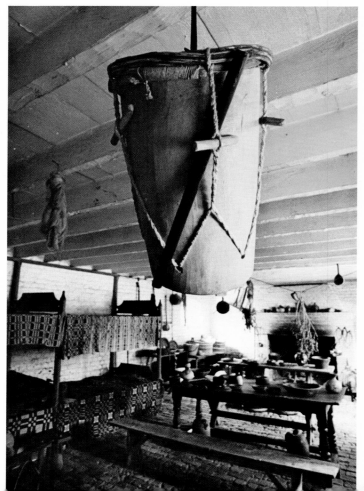

Despite its immorality, slavery was essential to
southern economic survival and accepted by plantation owners
—as chained slave figure embroidered on 1740s
bedspread suggests. Occasionally, an owner's will
manumitted—set free—a favored or deserving black, but
New England slavers were quick to supply replacements.
Slave life revolved around the work quarters,
fields, and simple houses. Left: Tool houses and slave
quarters at Mount Vernon. Below: "Slave street,"
also dating from 1740s, at Boone Hall, South Carolina.

Williamsburg, capital and seat of the royal governor, was the center of Virginia's social season. Activity heightened during meeting of the colonial assembly. Entire families moved to town. More remote planters built smaller versions of their plantation homes as town houses, and bordered them with gardens (l, r & bottom). Sons attended College of William and Mary (below), with patterned brick walks and building (possibly) by Christopher Wren.

Good Eating

Comfortable Settings, Historic Events: Apollo Room (above)
of Raleigh Tavern (center), where Virginia House of
Burgesses met as a provincial congress after being dissolved
by colonial governor for opposing Townshend duties.
Opposite: Christiana Campbell's Tavern has warm and comfortable
southern ambience. Sign (top) proclaims cuisine—which
included coastal sturgeon, planked shad, bluefish, oysters, clams,
crab, and shrimp—to Williamsburg passers-by.

George Washington of Virginia: His birthplace (above) at Wakefield on Northern Neck. Right: Contemporary transit, ax, and other equipment on family land where he made his first survey at age fifteen. Top: Miniature of Washington painted for wife Martha in 1776 by Charles Wilson Peale. Personal Effects: Pocket knives and field compass used in early surveys and in laying out of the streets of Alexandria.

Mount Vernon: "No estate in United America is more pleasantly situated
than this," wrote Washington of the Potomac view from his plantation manor,
which was his home for forty-five years. He was his own architect
for the colonnaded house (above), which was the center of a working farm
community that grew to 8,000 acres and supported itself on crops of corn,
wheat, and flax. Opposite: Martha Washington china and silver,
spurs presented by Washington to officer at Valley Forge,
Washington's riding crop, a dress sword, his deathbed.

5.
Religion

In colonial America church buildings were holy places, built with care and preserved with pride. A higher proportion of them survives from the 1600s and 1700s than of any other type of building. The first New England churches were the simplest of box-like houses, without bell, steeple, stained glass, or statuary. They remained simple throughout the years, but a growing pride in their appearance filled the congregations of eighteenth-century towns. By the late colonial period the meeting house fronted every village green, its slender spire rising above the surrounding houses, its white paint glistening against the dark foliage. To the side would be a burying ground, the granite and marble headstones cut with grieving inscriptions and, except in the oldest towns, not yet mellowed with age. In larger cities the church could be imposing indeed. Old South Church, North Church, and King's Chapel in Boston were grand structures.

In the South the soft-toned red brick of Anglican churches stands serenely along country roads or nestles into towns like Williamsburg, Annapolis, and Edenton. Worn to a smooth glow, communion silver brought from England is still to be found in older Episcopal churches, and many a home or church still has an age-battered eighteenth-century Bible in English, Dutch, German, or French.

Nor are the surviving churches, north or south, all of the Puritan or Anglican orthodoxies. One of the noblest religious edifices in America is the Touro Synagogue, built by the Sephardic Jews of colonial Newport, and designed by Peter Harrison, the same great architect who planned the King's Chapel. The Baptist meeting house is still one of the principal buildings of Providence. A small seventeenth-century Dutch Reformed Church huddles by the Sleepy Hollow Bridge, near Tarrytown, New York, where Ichabod Crane fled the Headless Horseman. The oldest church building in Philadelphia is Swedish Lutheran. Moravian churches in Bethlehem, Pennsylvania, and Salem, North Carolina, and Catholic churches in Philadelphia and rural Maryland all survive as testaments to religious variety.

Many of these colonial churches served dramatic public roles as well as religious ones. It was from Old South Church that Bostonians, dressed as Indians, emerged to empty British tea into Boston Harbor, and it was lanterns hung in the belfry of North Church that sped Paul Revere on his ride. Patrick Henry's "Give me liberty or give me death!" rang out to burgesses sitting in the pews of St. John's Church in Richmond.

The diversity of these old churches stands as evidence that in the American colonies men and women were freer to worship in ways not those of the state than anywhere in the western world. This freedom, however, was by no means complete. It was general for Protestants, far less so for Catholics and Jews. Yet there were significant numbers of Catholics in Maryland, Pennsylvania, and New York, and small congregations of Jews in Rhode Island and Pennsylvania, who were undisturbed in the practice of their religion.

Toleration was not equality. Except for Rhode Island and Pennsylvania every colony had an established church: Congregational in Massachusetts and Connecticut, Anglican elsewhere, and Dutch Reformed as well as Anglican in New York. Taxes were levied by the colonies for the support of these denominations on believer and nonbeliever alike. In the Anglican colonies many functions of local government were placed in the hands of parish vestries. For a period of New England's history church membership was a prerequisite to voting, and in the colonies generally officeholding was usually confined to Protestants.

A new idea was beginning to take form: that the government might simply be divorced from the church. It was far from universal acceptance. Not for two generations after the Revolution would the last state law establishing a religion be repealed. But in the practice of Rhode Island and Pennsylvania a precedent had been set that would be given national authority in the First Amendment to the Constitution and ultimately in the laws and constitutions of all the states.

The concept of the secular state did not arise from an indifference to religion, but from the very intensity with which the diverse faiths of the colonists were held. In Europe an established church was one of the pillars of the state. It was a means of binding the devotion of the people to their government. But in America, to identify the government with one faith was to alienate the zealous adherents of all others. Only a government neutral in religion could command the loyalty of all. This was one of the truly creative political ideas that emerged from the colonial experience.

Another was control of the church by laymen. The dissident Protestants—Congregationalists, Baptists, Quakers, Mennonites—were rebels against a hierarchy. For them the church did not transcend its members. Rather, it was the members banded together in a common faith who were the church. No bishop had authority over them and even the pastor was a leader chosen by the people, not a ruler imposed on them. Laymen dominated even the hierarchical Anglican Church in the colonies. There was no American bishop; and the Bishop of London, in whose diocese the colonies nominally fell, was a distant figure. The local parsons of the Anglican parishes were not usually men of great dignity and personal authority. There were almost no endowments, as in England, to provide for the support of the clergy. The rectors of parishes were financially dependent on their vestries, which were self-perpetuating bodies of local gentry. The vestry picked the parson, in conjunction with the assembly fixed his pay, and in general controlled the parish.

The ministers of the Congregational churches, though answerable to their deacons, were men of great influence and prestige. Many of them, like the Mathers, Jonathan Edwards, and Jonathan Mayhew, were among the towering figures of colonial New England. Similar positions of power and respect were enjoyed by the German pastors who led their flocks to the New World. But the Anglican rector often had a wretched time of it. The ablest of the young university graduates ordained in England rarely wanted to come to America; those who elected the colonies were more often than not those whose mediocre abilities and lack of connections allowed no other choices. Once in the colonies they often lived in near poverty. A meager income, frequently paid in inferior tobacco worth far less than its legally assigned value, had to be supplemented with the produce of a poor glebe. Frequently the parson had to keep a private school to make ends meet. It is perhaps not surprising that colonial rectors so often turned to wine and brandy as the solace of their poverty and frustration.

The public role of religion in America was almost the reverse of that in Europe. In the Old World the church was one of the ruler's instruments for control of his people, through which a hierarchy identified with the government imposed uniformity and exacted submission. In America the church was an instrument of the people themselves which, except for the Anglicans, embodied not their subordination to but their dissent from political authority.

Because membership and attendance were not generally compelled, a much higher proportion of the population of the colonies lived apart from any church than was the case in Great Britain or Europe. Indeed, in much of the back country settlers had no church to attend. Their only religious services came from itinerant ministers, sometimes fully ordained Methodists riding a regular circuit, sometimes wandering evangelists of doubtful sponsorship. The life these men led was hard, moving from settlement to settlement along frontier trails, their worldly goods no more than their saddlebags would hold. The ablest

Opening pages: Early Lutheran landmark in America was small, architecturally plain Augustus Church at Trappe, Pennsylvania, erected by its congregation in 1743. Only in Pennsylvania and Rhode Island was religious freedom guaranteed. Other colonies supported established churches.

preachers among them, however, might bring together a thousand or more listeners seated along a sloping hillside to hear a sermon full of doom and brimstone, but offering salvation from an eternity of torment. This sort of meeting in the open fields, the ancestor of the summer "revivals" and camp meetings of rural America, grew in importance with the westward spreading of settlement away from the established churches of the coastal areas.

But for those who voluntarily committed themselves to their faith, religion had a special intensity. Especially in the early days of New England, dedication to the Puritan faith illuminated the whole texture of life. Zeal waned, however, as the generations passed. The demands of the world were inexorable in a new land, the opportunities for gain enticing. The grandsons of the Puritan founders who came to build a new Canaan in the wilderness were building worldly farms and towns and fortunes, and assuming as familiar tradition the faith that had burned in their forefathers' hearts.

Eventually, in the 1730s and 1740s there came a Great Awakening. It began in western Massachusetts with the preaching of Jonathan Edwards, whose brilliant mind brought a new fervor to the old Puritan faith. It was spread from one end of the colonies to the other by George Whitefield, an English missionary who was perhaps the greatest preacher America has ever known, and by other evangelists. Throughout the country there was a revival of religious zeal expressed in outbursts of violent emotion. Puritanism was revivified. Conservative sects such as the Presbyterians were divided into New Lights, who accepted the evangelical revivalism, and the Old Lights who rejected it. The nearly dormant Baptist sect exploded into growth along the southern frontier. A new earnestness, expressed emotionally as well as intellectually, filled even the more traditional churches.

In part, the Great Awakening went hand-in-hand with the rise of pietism in Germany and an evangelical revival in England. John Wesley, for example, had his first pastoral experience in America as the very high-church and unsuccessful rector of a parish in Savannah. His failure to reach his parishioners and the contacts he made in Savannah with Moravian missionaries shattered his conservatism. The Moravians, like the other German sects described as pietist, paid scant attention to dogma and ritual. They saw as important only the simple piety of the individual worshipper in his own relationship to God. Upon his return to England, Wesley journeyed to the Continent to seek out the German pietist leaders, especially the Moravians. From their ideas, and from a revival of Puritan strains of thought in the Anglican Church, he formed his mature religious views. He became an ardent religious reformer, devoting his enormous energies to the creation of a Methodist Association—a body of totally committed Christians seeking to lead sinless lives. Though John Wesley never returned to America after his brief pastorate in Georgia, his ideas and followers came to the colonies to form the basis of the Methodist Church in America.

But another current flowed through the American mind in the eighteenth century. It was the same current, arising from the work of thinkers like Newton, Spinoza, and Leibniz, that created the European Enlightenment. Men whose minds were opened to this body of thought began to see God as a distant and impersonal force rather than as a Person, at once vengeful and loving. The Unitarian Church grew up in the midst of Congregationalism and attracted some of the finest minds of New England, such as John Adams. Other great men of the time, like Washington, continued a formal allegiance to a traditional faith, but hardly shared its dogma or its zeal. Still others, like Jefferson and Franklin, were active members of no denomination.

As this list of names indicates, the Revolution was to be led for the most part by men who adhered only formally to the traditional Christian faiths and who avoided religious enthusiasm. The religious mood of the founders of the Republic did not reflect the sermons of the evangelists of the Great Awakening, calling men away from the concerns of this world to look on the burning fires of Hell and aspire to the bliss of Heaven. Rather it reflected the cool detachment of the English and Scottish rationalist thinkers, who extended to religion the scientific and philosophical ideas of such men as Isaac Newton, John Locke, and David Hume. They rejected Calvinist belief in predestination and the intervention of God in the day-to-day workings of the universe. They thought of men as essentially good and perfectable, not inherently evil and damned but for the undeserved grace of God. They believed in the importance of an ethical life, rather than in sacraments and ritual, and they had an optimistic view of the human potential for progress.

The religious beliefs of the Revolutionary leaders would be expressed later in the refusal of the Constitutional Convention to open its sessions with prayer; in the Revolutionary movement toward the disestablishment of churches, culminating in the Virginia Statute for Religious Liberty drafted by Jefferson; and in the First Amendment to the Constitution denying to the Federal Government any role in matters of religion, whether to support or to restrict beliefs and observances.

And yet the dissident, democratic, Puritan character of colonial religion survived the Revolution and shaped its content. The Revolution was made by men whose forebears for generations had formed their own churches and committed themselves to their own beliefs, and who had not hesitated to defend those beliefs against hierarchy and authority. They had been brought up to believe not only that all men are created equal in the eyes of God, but that they retain an equal and direct responsibility to God, without the mediation of any earthly priest or ruler.

The idea of convenant was also one of the central concepts shared by the colonists of dissident sects. Men covenanted with each other to form a church. God covenanted with His elect to sustain and preserve them. When the signers of the Declaration of Independence pledged to each other their lives, their fortunes, and their sacred honor, they were covenanting in the tradition of their forebears back to the Mayflower Compact. The concept of a fundamental and unchangeable covenant as the basis of human association carried over to the drafting of state constitutions, one of the unique American contributions to political institutions, and ultimately to the creation of the Federal Constitution itself.

But the most important legacy to the Revolution from the religion of the colonists, and especially from the puritanical strain in all the sects, was a sense of earnest dedication to a divinely ordained cause beyond individual concerns. This did not disappear with a waning of belief in the God of Cotton Mather and Jonathan Edwards. It held together the core of the Continental army, half-paid, half-clothed, half-armed, through the bleak years of the war with Britain and sustained the earnest men who made the most serious and the most successful of the great revolutions.

Earliest Anglican (Episcopal) church still active in America is Bruton Parish Church of Williamsburg (above), completed in 1715. Congregation, led by Governor Spotswood, included councillors, burgesses, and "all classes of society." Jamestown communion service (top) came to Bruton when capital moved to Williamsburg. Baptismal font (opposite) stands on gravestone of Martha Washington's great-great grandfather, first rector of parish. Curved brickwork (r) was crafted by colonial masons.

New England Puritans founded the Congregational
Church as an independent institution controlled by
members who held themselves equal in the
sight of God. Each Congregationalist was bound
to interpret God's Word for himself, to
approach Him directly, to manage his own salvation.
Congregationalists kept their meeting
houses plain and simple, like Old Ship Meeting
House at Hingham, Massachusetts (r & below).
Worshipers in this unheated building
spent long Sundays listening to
two-hour sermons (timed by hourglass below) and
debating theological questions under the
guidance of ministers such as Ebenezer Gay
(l), who served at Old Ship for sixty-nine years.
Pastel sketch was done from life in 1750s.

Catholics were slow to gain a foothold in Protestant America. Only Maryland was founded as a Catholic haven, but Pennsylvania and Rhode Island were tolerant, as was the frontier, where Jesuit priests built chapels like that at Fort Niagara (l) for the comfort of traders and the conversion of Indians. Above & right: Touro Synagogue, in Newport, is oldest in country, was designed for descendants of Sephardic Jews, who arrived in 1660s, while Roger Williams still lived.

Society of Friends: Third Haven meeting house at Easton, Maryland (this page), built in 1684. Quakers were liberal English Puritans who found the Word of God in man's soul rather than in the Bible. No ministers were needed. All men were "friends" to be spoken to familiarly as "thee" and "thou." Right: Interior of Augustus Lutheran Church.

Preceding pages: Cloisters at Ephrata, Pennsylvania,
housed an austere, monastic religious community of Seventh-Day German
Baptists. Below left: Saal, where foot-washing rite was observed.
Right: Saron, or Sister House, a dining room for celebrating Lord's
Supper. Community was noted for illuminated musical scores.

Moravians were another German Protestant sect, like the Mennonites, Amish, and Seventh-Day Baptists. Established in America in 1735, Moravians were excellent musicians. Below left: Bethlehem, Pennsylvania, community church room, with traditional choir instruments. Right: Lamb of God weathervane, "sisters' house" for single women.

Central headstone in graveyard (opposite) is that of Ann Lee—"Mother Ann" or "Ann the Word"— founder of Shakers (1776) at Watervliet, New York. Pacifist, celibate, believing in equality of sexes, and common possession of goods, Shakers got name from fervor of worship. Rocking chair (at Fruitlands, Massachusetts) is Mother Ann's. This page: Steeple and interior of First Baptist meeting house built at Providence, Rhode Island, in 1775. This oldest Baptist congregation was founded by 1639 group that included Roger Williams. It held that individuals should not be baptized until they had accepted Christ after reaching age of reason.

6.
Way
of Life

The furniture, clothing, and tools of the first settlers were simple and utilitarian, even crude. There were few skilled craftsmen among the first-comers, and they found no market for luxurious products among their fellow colonists. At first even the most basic goods had to be imported from England: iron pots, axes, hoes, skirts and breeches. Until flocks of sheep and fields of flax could be established in the colonies, there was no raw material for household spinning and weaving. Blacksmiths had to await the discovery of native sources of iron ore before they could do more than mend or reshape the tools brought from England.

As the seventeenth century passed, however, colonial workmen began to flourish. The cost and risk of ocean shipping made imports extremely expensive, and months elapsed between the dispatch of an order to London and arrival of the goods. Colonists more willingly paid high prices for local furniture, silver, and ironwork that could be inspected before purchase and taken home as soon as it was ready. Responding to this opportunity, large numbers of craftsmen came to America.

English style became more graceful in the late seventeenth century, as the French fashions of the Restoration court of Charles II spread to the nobility and upper classes, replacing the massive designs of the Jacobean period. By the reign of Queen Anne (1702–15), the design of English furniture, silver, and china had entered a period of classic elegance that persisted for a century. During those same years a wealthy class emerged in the colonies, growing yearly in numbers and affluence. By the end of the colonial period the drawing rooms of the wealthy in Boston, New York, Philadelphia, and the plantation country rivaled in style and opulence all but the most magnificent homes of England.

Every large town in the northern colonies by then had dozens of cabinetmakers, fifty or more in Newport alone. They competently copied the simple elegance of the Queen Anne style and the later, more elaborate models of Chippendale and his contemporaries. But they modified these styles and introduced their own innovations, so that Boston chairs and Philadelphia and Hudson River designs became recognizable. In the South, which lacked cities capable of supporting large numbers of craftsmen, planters were more likely than northern merchants to continue importing their furniture from England; but even here skilled cabinetmakers flourished in such centers as Annapolis, Williamsburg, and Charleston.

Colonial silversmithing developed in the same way. As the colonists became prosperous they turned to London for imports of silver and eventually attracted skilled silversmiths to America. The earliest American products were simple spoons, porringers, and cups, which were produced in Boston as early as the 1650s. Colonial silver was not melted and poured in molds, but made into sheets, softened, hammered into the desired shape around a wooden mold, and finished with buffing, engraving, and polishing. It was a slow, painstaking, and difficult art, but one capable of creating pieces of great beauty.

The art of the silversmith was spurred by the increased use of tea, coffee, and chocolate, and a consequent demand for pots, pitchers, sugar bowls, creamers, and spoons. Much of the most charming work of the eighteenth century was in the production of these implements. The Huguenot smiths, who brought a uniquely French elegance to their work, included a skilled silver- and goldsmith named Apollos de Revoire, whose son, Paul Revere, was perhaps the greatest of the colonial workers in precious metals, as well as a distinguished patriot. His punch bowls, trays, coffee pots, tankards, and tableware are superb examples of a mature art.

The colonial silversmiths actually worked more extensively in pewter. Even the moderately well-to-do could afford it, and its soft glow survives in beautifully designed and proportioned tankards, bowls, and plates.

Blacksmiths were among the first of the colonies' artisans. Shoeing horses, making nails and hoes, axes and harness, and performing odd jobs of repair were essential to keeping the colonies going. And as the years passed, the smiths found increasing demand for ironwork of real artistry. Iron ore was abundant and easily reached, especially in the Pennsylvania hill country and the highlands of the Hudson. So was the hardwood needed to provide charcoal for smelting the ore. In England, meanwhile, forests were dwindling and mining the ever-deeper iron ore was becoming increasingly expensive. By the mid-eighteenth century the colonies had a surplus of pig iron that could be shipped to England, replacing imports from Sweden. In fact, so vigorous was the American iron industry that Parliament in 1750 passed an Iron Act which, though encouraging the continued production of colonial pig iron, forbade the construction of mills that might compete with British manufactures.

This did not deter the hundreds of colonial metalworkers, such as the German artisans who established the early Virginia ironworks at Germanna and the later immigrants to Pennsylvania who became master gunsmiths.

Glassmaking was one of the earliest industries attempted in the colonies, from the founding days of Jamestown itself. Though the colonial workmen never achieved the equivalent of fine French crystal, by the mid-eighteenth century they were producing bottles, jars, cruets, windowpanes, and tableware, including excellent and graceful stemware. Again the Pennsylvania Germans were the leaders.

Spinning and weaving were other very early colonial crafts. Cotton was still a luxury imported from Muslim India (muslin) through Calcutta (calico). The colonists' cloth was made of wool or linen, or a mixture called linsey-woolsey. Clothmaking began as soon as there were sheep and flax to provide fibers.

It was hard work. The sheep had to be sheared, the wool washed, dried, and combed in order to smooth and straighten the fibers. Only then could the spinning begin. Women filled any hours free of other chores with spinning skeins of wool into yarn, or yarn more tightly into thread. The early spinning wheels were precious imports from England, but in later years sturdy spinning wheels were a principal product of American cabinetmakers.

The preparation of linen thread was even more difficult than wool. After the flax was cut and the seeds threshed out, the stalks were placed in water until rotten. At this point, in an unpleasant and evil-smelling operation, the loosened fibers were removed and cleaned. These, too, were carded and combed, and then spun.

While spinning was done by women in their homes, heavy weaving was generally considered man's work and most of it was done by professional weavers. Looms were large and expensive pieces of equipment that might entirely fill a small room. They were operated by the weaver's hands and feet, and required strength as well as special skill. Farmers and townspeople brought yarn to the weaver to be made up into cloth. The larger plantations might have their own weaving houses, with several looms and slaves trained to operate them. By the mid-eighteenth century, when well-to-do ladies had more leisure, weaving became a fashionable occupation for them, especially the weaving of the more luxurious cloths. Crewel work, embroidery, and other forms of elegant needlework produced beautiful samplers, chair covers, and other decorative pieces.

Sturdy cloth for household use and everyday clothing was made in abundance by the end of the colonial period, but it remained a crude material. "Homespun" defined something simple and rough. The wealthy continued to import satin and silk and other fine fabrics for their best wear. As late as 1789,

Opening pages: Rigors of pioneering Puritan life were eased by a variety and abundance of food unknown to similar social levels in England. Table at Harlow House at Plymouth is laden with dishes nourishing to early New England: turkey, cranberries, clams and mussels, cider, Indian pudding.

George Washington was thought to have taken a bold and pioneering step in support of America's infant industry when he wore a suit of brown Connecticut broadcloth for his inauguration as president.

Here and there in the larger towns were quality tailors, dressmakers, and milliners ready to cater to expensive tastes with clothes made in the latest London fashion, almost always with imported fabrics and laces. As models they showed little dolls dressed in replicas of the current London and Paris styles. A companion luxury industry was the making of wigs and perukes for ladies and gentlemen, whom fashion still required on formal occasions to appear bewigged and powdered.

Heating and lighting even the most elegant homes presented formidable problems. Toward the end of the colonial period the use of stoves was spreading, and the cast-iron fireplace type invented by Ben Franklin was proving to be an efficient if somewhat unlovely device. But open fireplaces remained the principal source of heat even to the end of the period. These were a wretched way to warm a room, often smoky and fitful, burning the face and leaving the rear to freeze, and never reaching to the corners.

Except in great homes with many servants, fires were kept going only in the kitchen and parlor or family living room. Bedrooms were likely to be left in their winter chill. Well-to-do families might have bedwarmers—covered brass pans with a long handle. These were filled with hot coals from the fireplace and passed over the freezing bed sheets to warm them for a flannel-gowned shiverer.

The oil lamp with glass chimney that brought light to nineteenth-century homes was not invented until the 1780s. Throughout the colonial period homes were lit by firelight, rushes, rag lamps, or candles. Resinous splinters of decaying pine—lightwood—might be stuck in a holder by the fireplace, or twisted rags or dried rushes might be placed in a pan of oil or fat to serve as a wick. None of these was a really satisfactory method of illumination.

Candles were much better, but they were expensive. The most sought-after, and scarcest, candle material was spermaceti—whale oil. The wax from bayberries and other plants gave a less brilliant light but a pleasing odor. Most candles for everyday use, however, were made from tallow, the fat saved from beef and mutton.

Aside from cost, all candles were used stingily because any large number of them also produced enough heat, smoke, and stench to make a room uninhabitable. Even wealthy colonials ate and read and did needlework in little pools of light penetrating the shadowy darkness of their houses.

By the end of the colonial period, in such centers as Boston, New York, Philadelphia, Williamsburg, and Charleston, one could buy most of the products that could be bought in London itself. If they were fewer in quantity and a shade less fancy than the finest London work, they nevertheless represented varied and excellent workmanship.

The craftsmen who produced so much utility and beauty were drawn to America by the freedom and dignity of life it offered, as well as by the high wages their skills could command. A draftsman in America was not a menial as in Europe. He might, like Paul Revere or Benjamin Franklin, become a famous figure and leading citizen. If he was competent, diligent, and prudent, he was sure to be financially comfortable and might become wealthy.

Eventually, however, more and more of the best craftsmen were native Americans trained in the colonies. They learned their trade by apprenticeship, as in Europe, though the demand for skilled workmen led to constant pressure to reduce the period of indenture from seven years to four, or even three. Nor were there guilds in the colonies as there were in Britain and on the Continent to enforce high standards of materials and workmanship, and to insist on confining the work of each guild to its members. On the frontier, and indeed everywhere outside the larger towns, Americans were forced to be jacks of many trades. A frontiersman was his own carpenter, mason, and blacksmith; his wife her own spinner, weaver, tailor, candlemaker, soapmaker, apothecary, and physician. Even the skilled craftsmen in the large towns had to be versatile. An expert cabinetmaker might turn out kitchen tables on demand and the finest builder erect stables in addition to mansions. The man who painted the parlor walls might daub the portrait of the mistress of the house.

The yeastiness of colonial life showed in all its handiwork. An exuberance of style combined with functional practicality. A readiness to make do with materials at hand and with rough-and-ready skills strained against a desire for excellence and a naïve pride in visible elegance. The standards and the models were English, but the objects created were very American in their simplicity and strength.

The American transformation of English prototypes carried into the kitchen too. British cooking of the seventeenth and eighteenth centuries did not have the bland dullness of the Victorian table. It was hearty with beef and game, and zesty with spice—meals, as was later said, to "make a hungry man thank God for the room there was in him." It was this tradition that simmered in the American kitchen, with modifications depending on the foodstuffs available. Beef was tougher, game more abundant, pork plentiful. Squash and other vegetables domesticated by the Indians added variety. But the greatest innovation of the colonial kitchen was the use of Indian corn.

The Indians were superb agriculturalists and they originally domesticated many of the crops that are now basic to world agriculture. But the most important of their contributions was corn. It is hard to see how the first colonies could have survived, or the swift westward movement have succeeded, without this amazing grain. Wheat and barley were demanding crops, thriving only in fertile soils that had been thoroughly cleared and deeply plowed. In the earliest settlements and along the frontier there was no time to clear the fields fully. There were few plows and fewer draft animals to pull them. Men had to work the fields with hoes.

But for corn this was enough. It thrived almost anywhere and returned a generous yield. Beans and squash could be grown along with it in the same fields. Corn itself could be ground to make meal from which johnnycake and corn pone were baked to become the breadstuffs of the frontier. Parched grains of corn could be kept for weeks and carried by a hunter or traveler. With the tough coating of the grains soaked off by lye, corn became hominy or could be ground as grits. Fresh corn on the cob, boiled or roasted, was a favorite food. Cooked with lima beans it became the Indian standby—succotash. Sweetened with sugar or molasses, corn-meal mush became a dessert as Indian pudding. The stalks were fodder for cattle, the dried cobs were kindling for fires and bowls for pipes.

Perhaps the greatest Indian contribution after corn itself was the use of the wild turkey as food. From the earliest days of the colonies this magnificent bird was the symbol of feasting. Roasted and stuffed with oysters or sausages, surrounded with corn and parsnips, turnips and peas, beans and sweet potatoes, pickled peaches and watermelon rind, and followed with half a dozen pies and cakes, the turkey was the center of holidays and celebrations.

Abundance perhaps marked the greatest difference between food in the Old World and the New. Hunger was the companion of the poor throughout Europe, and a dull meagerness of diet was the common condition even of those who avoided hunger itself. America offered a sufficiency for all. At the simplest level, the cornucopia of the colonial kitchen symbolized the New World to those who came to reap its fullness.

Kitchen fireplace—for heating, cooking,
and sometimes lighting—was the hub of early
colonial house. Indian corn, ground
into meal, roasted green, or hulled and dried
as hominy, was the basic diet.
Indian squash and
pumpkin were other native vegetables.
Meat may have been wild game, local pork
or beef, or shellfish gathered by children.
Left: Kitchen of Warren House re-created
at Plimouth Plantation.
Above: Hearth utensils at Washington's
Valley Forge headquarters,
with Martha Washington tea kettle.
Above right: Indian pudding.
Right: Corn bread.

*Life among the well-to-do was blessed with creature
comforts. Top: Imported china at Mount Vernon and pewter tableware
in sideboard at Williamsburg. Above: Dairy at Philipsburg Manor
was a cool room for preservation of milk and cheeses. Right:
Pomander balls of citrus fruits and spices freshened the air.*

Prosperity brought comfort and even elegance to southern home life in 1700s. Williamsburg imported great cones of Caribbean sugar (top) which were crumbled for use with tongs. Gardening became fashionable and many Williamsburg homes had separate garden houses (l & above). Self-sufficient plantations developed their own life style. Breakfast at Stratford (r) was at ten, included cold roasts, smoked ham, hot hash, bread, drinks.

For the wealthy, dining became more elaborate and stylized. At Gunston Hall (opposite) George Mason favored a table laid in precise and symmetrical English fashion—with Potomac shad on the platter. Ladies of quality sometimes served tea in their bedchamber, as at Kenmore (above), home of Washington's sister at Fredericksburg, Virginia. At Van Cortlandt Manor (l), on the Hudson River, the wine-glass rinser was Dutch Delftware.

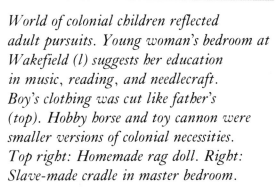

World of colonial children reflected
adult pursuits. Young woman's bedroom at
Wakefield (l) suggests her education
in music, reading, and needlecraft.
Boy's clothing was cut like father's
(top). Hobby horse and toy cannon were
smaller versions of colonial necessities.
Top right: Homemade rag doll. Right:
Slave-made cradle in master bedroom.

Towns the size of Williamsburg drew large numbers of shopkeepers and craftsmen, each with his distinctive sign. Clockwise, from tailor's fleecy lamb, are bootmaker, butcher, silversmith, tea and spice seller. Imports—from latest London fashions (in store window, opposite) to tropical citrus fruits—were available to satisfy 18th century's taste for luxury. Newspapers appeared. Dancing masters and theater troupes toured the towns. Puppet shows and fairs were entertainment for all.

In 18th-century America, about one man in five was a
craftsman. The colonies offered a ready market for their
products and good opportunities to rise in status and wealth.
The wigmaker (opposite), gratifying a fashion started
at the French court, displayed his wares on blockheads—
from which the pejorative term derived. Pasteur-Galt Apothecary
Shop (above) was run by two physicians of those names, who
could handle surgical instruments, compound ointments
and elixirs, and manipulate pill-roller on counter.

A boot- and shoemaker's shop (l)
and silversmith's. Superb work like
goblet, bowl, and candle snuffers
(r) gave silversmiths (such as
Paul Revere) the highest social rank
among colonial artisans. They
worked Spanish pieces of eight and
other silver coins into tableware
which eventually achieved a simple,
beautifully proportioned American
style unequaled since.

Cooper (opposite) probably was most numerous artisan in colonial America, the ironmonger (l) the most important. Buckets and barrels were needed for transporting salt meat, whiskey, and other frontier products to market. Blacksmiths' tools, utensils, and household hardware were vital to every enterprise. Makers of musical instruments (above) were rare, but usually were artists in inlay and veneer, as well as in the temper of clavichords.

157

Illumination always was a problem. All fuels smoked, smelled, made a mess, or burned too feebly. And candles (being built up by dipping, at right) were expensive. Clockwise, from left, above: a candle reflector, two kinds of candleholders, a "betty" lamp (containing liquid oil and wick), a rare wooden candle lantern.

7.
The King's Men

The governors of Rhode Island and Connecticut were elected by the settlers; those of Pennsylvania and Maryland were named by the proprietors. The governors of all the other colonies during the eighteenth century were the king's men. Thousands of miles from Britain—a voyage of weeks by infrequent sailing ship—the king's men represented on the frontiers of empire the dignity and authority of a distant throne.

The responsibilities of the governor were great. He represented the authority not only of the Crown, but of Parliament. He was charged with preserving and asserting the power of the homeland over its American possessions. At the same time he was expected to regard and protect the interests and rights of the colonists. He was responsible for defending them against Indians and foreign invaders. His other duties included keeping the peace, enforcing the law, administering justice, and initiating the construction of roads, fortifications, and public buildings.

Awesome legal authority was vested in the king's man. The governor could convene and prorogue the colonial assembly and call for new elections. No law could go into effect without his approval, and he could suspend that approval while an act was submitted to the king for acceptance or veto. He sat as the head of the Governor's Council, whose members were usually named on his recommendation. He appointed sheriffs and other lesser officers of the Crown and commanded such armed forces as the colony might have. He could call out the local militia and was responsible for its training.

The Council was not only an executive and legislative body; it was also the colony's highest court, and the governor thereby combined judicial authority with his executive and legislative roles.

Though the Crown gave the governors sweeping authority it was stingy with the means of power. No money went with the responsibility. To run the colonial government, even to pay his own salary and expenses, the governor had to depend on funds raised by local taxation and voted by the colonial assembly. Almost never did the governor have regular British troops at his command. To defend the colony, to maintain order, and put down riots he had to depend almost entirely on the local militia. Laws could be enacted only by the vote of an elected assembly and they could be enforced only by popular consent. Whatever the language of his commission or his instructions from the Crown, the governor had little real power.

It is surprising that, faced with all these difficulties, so many governors were both successful and popular. Most of them were landless and often moneyless younger sons of noble families or of the landed gentry in Britain. More often than not they had been career army officers. The more enterprising governors were resolute and energetic men, very loyal to Britain and to the Crown. They were avid for wealth, and most of them sought colonial appointments hoping to earn enough from land grants, investments, salary, and fees to maintain and even improve on the style of life they had known at home.

However sturdy in defense of their interests in the assemblies, the colonists were deferential toward the Crown itself. The governor's principal strength was in his role as the local embodiment of the king's majesty. The royal governors tried to reflect this glory in the way they lived. They dressed smartly, entertained lavishly, traveled in a coach-and-four, and opened sessions of the assembly with a small-scale imitation of the pomp with which the king opened Parliament.

Alexander Spotswood was the queen's man, then the king's, in Virginia from 1710 to 1722. A professional soldier, like so many governors, he had been wounded at the Battle of Blenheim fighting under the Duke of Marlborough. When he came to Virginia as governor (actually as lieutenant governor under a titular governor), he was a young man of thirty-four. Williamsburg was a raw village which had been made the colonial capital a dozen years before but still lacked imposing public buildings.

In 1706 the Virginia Assembly finally voted to build a governor's palace, fifty-four by forty-eight feet, two stories, slate-roofed, with separate buildings for kitchen and stables. Spotswood personally oversaw the completion of the building, which was half-finished when he arrived. He was determined to make it a truly impressive symbol of royal magnificence and he succeeded. It was a beautiful brick structure, an early form of the architecture which has come to be known as Georgian. Separate flanking buildings provided an office for the governor and a guardhouse. Magnificent formal gardens stretched back to a fish pond. The building spoke in stately form of wealth and power, and must have been awesome to the countrymen and burgesses who came to Williamsburg when the Assembly sat.

Spotswood's term of office was nearly over when the palace was finished, but it remained a monument to his energy and taste. The same energy was shown by his pressure to expand the colony westward, by the expedition he led to the Blue Ridge and the Valley of the Shenandoah, and by the establishment of an iron industry. He was recalled to England in 1722, but he had fallen in love with Virginia. After a belated marriage he returned to the colony in 1730 as assistant postmaster general for the colonies, and lived out the rest of his life at his country estate near the ironworks at Germanna.

His palace housed a succession of notable king's men, including the last of the royal governors. Two of the people's men—Patrick Henry and Thomas Jefferson—resided there as elected governors before the building was destroyed by fire in 1781. The present reconstruction, begun in 1930, recreates the palace as it was at the height of its glory.

Another outstanding king's man, typi-cal of the professional administrators of the later colonial period, was William Tryon. Born in 1729, he was the well-connected grandson of an earl, but like other landless descendants of the aristocracy had to find his career in the army. After thirteen years' service, he was appointed lieutenant governor of North Carolina in 1764 and governor the next year.

North Carolina during Tryon's administration was the fastest growing of the colonies, as tens of thousands of German and Scotch-Irish families poured into the back country. Tryon was sympathetic to their needs, urged the creation of new western counties, personally led an expedition into the mountains to demark a line separating the white settlements from the Cherokee lands, and strove—vainly—to persuade the Crown to charter a college at Charlotte for the western settlements.

Nevertheless, tensions rose between the eastern counties and the back country, which felt underrepresented and overtaxed and in general ill served by the colonial government. Armed bands of western farmers calling themselves "Regulators" formed to resist the exactions of judges, sheriffs, and tax collectors they thought corrupt, and took over the court and county government. Tryon led the militia against the Regulators and defeated them in the Battle of Alamance in 1771, restoring peace to the colony.

One of the grievances that provoked the Regulators' uprising was the tax levy to pay for "Tryon's Palace," a residence and office for the governor in the newly selected capital at New Bern. This was a structure even larger and more imposing than the governor's palace at Williamsburg and was considered the finest public building in all the colonies. But after the capital was moved to Raleigh in 1792 the palace rapidly deteriorated. In the 1950s the entire structure was rebuilt on the original foundations in a meticulous restoration that recalls, as does the governor's palace of Williamsburg, the majesty of England's final days of rule in America.

Opening pages: Sumptuous office of Governor William Tryon in Tryon's Palace at New Bern, North Carolina, was a typically splendid setting for king's men representing power of the Crown in the colonies. Tryon's militia beat down farmers and frontiersmen protesting unjust taxation and extortion in 1771.

Chamber of governor's council at Williamsburg, from which landed aristocracy effectively controlled Virginia through its privileged position as advisor to the governor on matters of law, taxation, and public policy. Other colonies were similarly dominated. Above: Rampant lion, symbol of British crown atop State House in Boston.

London expected colonial governors to live on a scale
commensurate with their importance as representatives of the
king, but provided no funds, no troops, no officialdom.
Governors relied on their own ingenuity and whatever taxes they
could exact. Most did well enough. Governor Botetourt of
Virginia noted in 1769: "Fifty-two dined with me
yesterday, and I expect at least that number today."
Opposite: Master bedroom in Governor's Palace at Williamsburg
and silver communion service presented to College
of William and Mary by another governor, William Gooch.
Below left: Dining room at Tryon's Palace; reception
room and solid silver chamber pots at Williamsburg.

Reconstructed governor's palaces at Williamsburg (l) and New Bern (below & r). An account published in London in 1724 describes Williamsburg as "a magnificent structure built at the publick expense . . . beautified with gates, fine gardens, offices, walks, a fine canal, orchards, etc. with a great number of the best arms nicely posited, by the ingenious contrivance of the most accomplished Colonel [Governor] Spotswood."

8.
The
Frontier

A new breed of American developed in the eighteenth century—the frontiersman. Single men and single families ventured into the forest to gain land and livelihood. Beyond the reach of easy trade with the East, they had to provide for themselves. More often than not they ignored land titles and settled where they wished; surveyors and county courts were far away. The pioneers lived by rifle and musket, meanwhile clearing a few acres in rough fashion by girdling the trees and leaving them to die. When the sun could penetrate the leafless branches they planted corn among the decaying trunks and built rude cabins.

As the years passed, some stayed on to clear more acres, grub out the stumps, get a valid land title, build a substantial house, bring the plow to earth that had known only the hoe, and at last integrate with the settled area to the east. Others, weary of the irksome labor of clearing and breaking the land, sold their dubious titles, their half-opened fields, and their cabins, and moved west to repeat the process. They had married the forest and become frontiersmen.

Most of these men and women were part of a flood of new migration that poured over the piedmont and pressed against the mountains in the half-century before the Revolution. Angular Presbyterian Scotch-Irish from Ulster and displaced German peasants from the Rhineland arrived by endless shiploads, principally at the port of Philadelphia. As the Pennsylvania back lands were filled, these immigrants spilled down the Valley of Virginia and flowed out across the Carolina and Georgia piedmont.

The life they lived was different from that of even the earliest days in the coastal settlements. The Atlantic was a roadway as well as a barrier, and goods could be shipped more cheaply from London to the Chesapeake than from the Chesapeake to the farms beyond the Blue Ridge. The earliest settlers were sustained for years by shipments from England; and from their first days in the New World they spent much of their strength finding and producing materials to send to England in exchange for products they needed or wanted. This was not possible for the forest-bound frontiersmen. Without passable roads or navigable streams, they were more effectively cut off from the coast than the coast was from Europe. They had to find their own living, depending on the tidewater only for guns, powder, and shot, or for an occasional iron pot, hoe, or ax. Surpluses of food or grain were too expensive to ship to the tidewater unless they could be sent as whiskey, or as live cattle or hogs that could be walked to market.

The frontiersmen fed themselves by hunting and fishing and growing patches of corn, much as had their Indian predecessors. They became skilled woodsmen and riflemen, able handlers of an ax. They raised hogs and scrub cattle that could feed themselves in the forest. Annual roundups were held, as in the later West, to sort and brand the new calves. The tough beef supplemented meat from the deer, turkeys, and rabbits that fell to the frontiersman's rifle. Cornhusk mattresses, rude tables, and homemade benches furnished the cabins, which were built of logs or split planks.

The settlers moved west faster than the church, faster than schools, newspapers, or government. The men were an unlettered, brawling lot. Itinerant evangelists might stir them to religious frenzy during an annual revival meeting, but there was rarely a church for them to attend throughout the year. Colonial governments, firmly in the hands of coastal farmers and townsmen, were slow to create counties on the frontier which would be eligible to send representatives to the Assembly. Throughout the colonial period, the back country was seriously underrepresented in the colonial capitals.

The refusal to create new counties, or to create them rapidly enough, meant that westerners had to make long journeys over half-cleared roads to register deeds or land claims, file suits, or carry on other legal business. They also found the assemblies negligent in providing protection against the Indians, who were again becoming aggressive as advancing settlers threatened their hunting grounds. The only government agent much in evidence, westerners felt, was the tax collector, and they bitterly resented the levies exacted from their small store of hard cash. Eventually, almost every colony was torn by tensions between the old settlements along the coast and the westerners pressing against the mountains.

The surge westward did not escape the notice of land speculators—among them money-hungry colonial governors and their wealthy friends—who now began to look beyond the mountains. Traders had long since penetrated those barriers and gained for Pennsylvania and Virginia some of the Ohio Valley furs that normally went to the French or, through the Iroquois, to the English merchants at Albany. These adventurers were aware of the abundance of fertile land that lay along the Ohio and its upper tributaries. Many years would pass before there were men and resources to clear and settle this broad domain, but farsighted land speculators wanted to be on hand when settlers arrived and to greet them with offers of deeds.

The western boundaries of most of the thirteen colonies were vague, mostly through ignorance of the continent's vast geography. Royal charters, written in Europe by men who thought the Pacific lapped the western slopes of the Appalachian Mountains, usually granted land "from sea to sea." Virginia's charter was even more expansive. It went not only from sea to sea, but "west and northwest." The reference to "northwest" became the basis for Virginia's claims to what are now Ohio, Indiana, Illinois, and Michigan—in addition to the territory, now West Virginia and Kentucky, that was unquestionably within its borders. Pennsylvania and Connecticut also asserted claims to territory west of the mountains and north of the Ohio. But it was Virginia,

the wealthiest and most powerful of the colonies, which most aggressively asserted its pretensions. In 1748, at the close of King George's War (the American phase of Europe's War of the Austrian Succession), when the French had been battered a bit and the imperial appetites of English colonists whetted, a number of leading Virginians organized the Ohio Company to settle and develop the lands beyond the mountains. From the governor of Virginia they received a grant of two hundred thousand acres (about three hundred square miles) which could be selected anywhere in the Ohio Valley.

The stirring of English interest in the valley aroused the French and the Indians as well. For more than a century and a half French voyageurs from Montreal had navigated the Great Lakes and the streams flowing into Lake Erie to trade with the Indians for their rich annual catch of furs. They had no interest in settling the area for themselves, but they were determined to bar the English from interfering with the fur trade. The Indians were well aware of the difference between the French traders and the English farmers who wanted their lands. They became increasingly restless as the first English trickled through the mountain passes.

The key to the west was the forks of the Ohio (the present site of Pittsburgh). The streams that joined there to form the Ohio reached toward French Canada to the north and Virginia to the south. The Ohio itself formed an easy route to the rich, vast, unsettled valley of the Mississippi.

Both French and English realized the strategic value of the forks, and in 1753 French troops began to move from the Great Lakes to secure the area. The governor of Virginia, alarmed at this threat to the interests of his friends who owned the Ohio Company, hastened to respond. He picked a young surveyor used to the western woods, a twenty-one-year-old named Washington, and sent him through the winter wilderness to warn the French that they

Opening pages: Fort Niagara, at strategic junction of Lake Ontario and the Niagara River in Upper New York, was crucial to French role in fur trade with Indians. It was captured by British under Sir William Johnson in 1759, at end of French and Indian Wars. British built blockhouse at right.

were entering territory claimed by His Majesty's colony of Virginia. Washington made the difficult journey, picked a promising site for a fort at the forks, and ascended the Allegheny until he reached the French forces. Its commander received him politely and assured him that it was the English who were trespassing the lands of His Most Christian Majesty, the King of France. Washington, realizing the contest for the West was now joined, made a desperate journey back to Virginia, forcing his way through blizzards, swimming an ice-filled river, riding horses to their death on the snow-burdened trails. The Virginia government moved immediately to fortify the forks. It was summer before an expedition could be dispatched, but at last a body of Virginia militia, plus some royal troops from South Carolina, started hacking a road.

They came too late. Reinforced French troops had already seized the forks and built a strong post they named Fort Duquesne. Washington, second in command of the little expedition at the outset, had become its leader when the original commander, Joshua Fry, died on the march. He realized it was impossible to capture Fort Duquesne and after a brief skirmish with an advance party of French he hurriedly threw up fortifications of his own. He called the little post Fort Necessity, and here he awaited French attack. It came quickly. Washington and his men were soundly beaten and forced to surrender on July 4, 1754. Released in humiliation, he led his bedraggled troops back to Virginia. The French were left in control of the West.

Neither the French nor the British were yet ready to engage in full-scale war for the unsettled western wilderness. But each was determined to hold what it regarded as its own. Britain sent to America one of its ablest professional soldiers, Major General Edward Braddock, with a body of British redcoats to match the white-uniformed French regulars. Braddock arranged to send William Johnson,

a powerful trader who had close contacts with the Iroquois, up the Hudson in the hope of capturing Crown Point, the French fort on Lake Champlain that barred the principal route to Montreal. Governor William Shirley of Massachusetts was ordered to establish a fortified post at Oswego, on the southern shore of Lake Erie, and to take the French post at Niagara, the main supply depot in the Ohio Valley.

All of these expeditions failed. Shirley reached and fortified Oswego, but too late in the season to attack Niagara. Johnson reached and fortified the southern end of Lake George, but proceeded no further. Braddock and his men painfully cut a road across the mountains from what is now Cumberland, Maryland, to the environs of Fort Duquesne. George Washington, now a proud young man of twenty-three, eager to become a regular officer in the British army, accompanied Braddock but only as an unpaid volunteer aide.

In July, 1755, as they approached their goal, the advance body of Braddock's army stumbled into a party of Indians and French regulars, who caught the British strung out at a ford. Murderous fire from French and Indians hidden in the forest killed Braddock and other senior British officers and finally threw the redcoats into headlong retreat. Two horses were shot from under Washington, but miraculously he escaped unwounded. The rest of the British army rapidly retreated and took up quarters in the safety of Philadelphia.

Indians, incited and armed by the French, now mercilessly attacked the English traders and pioneers beyond the mountains and even in the Shenandoah Valley, driving them back to the piedmont. The whole frontier lay defenseless before the tribesmen.

During these two years of frontier battles, France and England were officially at peace. But in 1756 the Seven Years War began. This pitted Great Britain and Prussia against France, Spain, Austria, and Russia in a titanic battle for empire. The principal opponents, France and Britain, were locked in war in Europe and Asia, the Caribbean and the Mediterranean, as well as in North America. It was truly the first world war.

For two years the war went badly for the British, but during 1757 a new hero came to power as Prime Minister of England: William Pitt, who threw all of Britain's wealth and power into a total war for world dominance. The results showed in 1758. In Nova Scotia, strategic Fort Louisburg fell to the British, opening the St. Lawrence. French merchant ships were swept from the seas, leaving French troops in Canada without supplies. A new British force cut a road directly across the mountains of Pennsylvania, a more direct route than Braddock's, and easily captured Fort Duquesne, which was renamed Fort Pitt.

The British momentum was sustained. In 1759 William Johnson took Fort Niagara, completely closing the French routes to the Ohio Valley. Jeffrey Amherst captured Ticonderoga and Crown Point, and moved north to Quebec. General James Wolfe's army, moving up the St. Lawrence, joined Amherst's forces. In the climactic battle of the war, Quebec, the capital of Canada, was taken. In September of the following year Montreal, the last French stronghold, surrendered.

The war was over in America, though the formal peace did not come until 1763, when Britain had triumphed across the world. In the Treaty of Paris of that year, France surrendered Canada and recognized Great Britain's claim to all the land from the mountains to the Mississippi. To her ally, Spain, in compensation for losses elsewhere, France ceded New Orleans and all her claims to lands west of the Mississippi. Save for a few tiny islands, France's total American empire had been lost.

But the West was not yet open to the American colonists. The Indians of the Ohio Valley were now left without French support to face the prospect of a growing flood of settlers driving them from their lands. Foreseeing their peril they organized themselves in a united and desperate effort to drive the English back across the mountains. This effort was called Pontiac's Conspiracy, after its inspired leader. It failed, as all Indian efforts to defend their homelands eventually failed, but not before an initial bloody success in freeing much of the eastern Ohio Valley from white intruders.

In large part to reassure the Indians, the British government in 1763 established a Proclamation Line running along the crest of the Alleghenies which reserved lands west of the line for the tribes. But one might as well have tried to dam the tides. In 1768 the Iroquois undertook to cede lands not really theirs around the Cumberland Gap and in eastern Kentucky, in each case trying to direct an inevitable white migration away from their own heartlands.

In the years between 1768 and the Revolution a stream of settlers moved steadily over the old roads to Fort Pitt and the upper Ohio. Another stream moved up the Shenandoah Valley into what is now eastern Tennessee and through the Cumberland Gap into Kentucky. Indians had drawn back from these areas and for a few years the settlers were free of the fear of attack from either the French or the Indians. New settlements multiplied. The British authorities made some effort to slow the pace and protect the unceded lands. But as Lord Dunmore, the governor of Virginia, wrote: "I have learnt from experience that the established authority of any government in America and the policy of government at home are both insufficient to restrain the Americans; and that they do and will remove as their avidity and restlessness incite them. They acquire no attachment to place; but wandering about seems engrafted in their nature; and it is a weakness incident to it, that they should ever imagine the lands further off are still better than those upon which they are already settled."

*Sharpening rivalry for the American West
in 1750s centered on upper Ohio valley. To forestall
British expansion, French turned fur-trading
post of Fort Niagara (below) into an
elaborate stronghold with new earthworks and
artillery batteries, established Fort Duquesne
at the strategic forks of the Ohio
River, and fortified Crown Point and
Ticonderoga (r) on Lake Champlain.*

1754: When Major George Washington,
heading a small British expeditionary force,
learned that French had captured forks
of the Ohio, he built little Fort
Necessity (bottom l) at Great Meadows
in western Pennsylvania. A
French force overwhelmed him and burned the
fort, but released him after surrender.
1755: British General Edward Braddock attempted
conquest of Fort Duquesne by cutting 110-mile
wagon road through wilderness (below),
was ambushed and killed by French and Indians.
1758: Fort Ligonier was strongpoint along
route of General John Forbes, who
finally captured Duquesne. Pictures: Spiked
bastion, Forbes's field gear in reproduction
hut, barracks, hospital, and storeroom.

British regulars and Iroquois warriors under Sir William Johnson, British Indian commissioner, captured Niagara in 1759, as General James Wolfe defeated French on Plains of Abraham, outside Quebec city. French attempt to recapture *Quebec* in next year failed and all Canada was surrendered to British. In 1764, Indian Agent Johnson invited northern tribes to fort (through Gate of Five Nations, above) for meetings in council room (r), persuaded them to join British cause.

9.
Political
Prelude

to pass

without any

Ship appea

Subjects

Our. H

SHILLING • HALF • PENNY

VI · PENCE

Lor

When the Treaty of Paris was signed in 1763, Great Britain was at the height of its glory. The subcontinent of India, all of Canada, Florida, and the American West from the Appalachians to the Mississippi had been added to its Empire. Its military and naval power was unrivaled. Its new young king, George III, an earnest and devoted ruler, commanded enthusiastic loyalty. Yet within a dozen years the Americans would be in armed rebellion, and twenty years after the first a second Treaty of Paris would seal the loss of thirteen American colonies, the Empire's brightest jewels.

What went wrong? For a century and a half, Britain and the colonies had maintained an affectionate if sometimes quarrelsome relationship. A bond of common loyalties had made it unnecessary to support British rule with British arms in America. Britons and colonists had fought side by side in four wars against the French in the New World. No Englishmen were prouder of English traditions and liberties than those who were born and reared in America.

Yet, paradoxically, it was the triumph of the Empire that led to its disruption. In earlier decades Britain had viewed its American possessions with indifference. Seventeenth-century England was torn by internal struggles; in the eighteenth it was enraptured by growing mercantile and agricultural wealth. The first two Georges, who reigned from 1715 to 1760, were content to leave issues of policy to a succession of able Whig ministers who, in turn, believed in letting the American commonwealths rule themselves with only nominal imperial control.

Victory in the Seven Years War for empire ended all that. Decisions of imperial scope had to be made: How were the new dominions—from India to the trans-Appalachian West—to be governed and defended? How was trade to be regulated? How was the whole imperial enterprise to be financed?

Such decisions would have a major impact on the colonies, yet none of them could be made by a colonial assembly acting alone. The new Empire needed a central imperial government.

George III and his newly appointed ministers never doubted that Parliament and the Crown was just such a government. Determined to strengthen parliamentary power, George III—and George Grenville, his prime minister—devised a policy of restraints and controls which checked the growing independence of the American colonies. Americans were alarmed and embittered by this peremptory exercise of authority, but what aroused them to open resistance were the efforts of the king's ministers to levy taxes by act of Parliament. The first, in 1765, was the Stamp Tax. Patterned after a British tax, it required stamps of varying value to be placed on newspapers, tavern licenses, college diplomas, ships' papers, court documents, playing cards, and indeed on virtually every paper of any significance whatever. To Grenville and his colleagues it seemed an entirely reasonable measure. Britons were vastly more heavily taxed than Americans, and the sums raised were all to be spent for the government of the colonies.

But Americans saw themselves being taxed by a Parliament in which they were not represented. Conceding Parliament's right to do this would be to abandon themselves to the control of an alien establishment, without rights Parliament or the British governors were bound to respect. Their reaction was violent. In August a Boston mob descended on the home of Andrew Oliver, the Stamp Tax collector for Massachusetts, and wrecked it. It moved on to his office and destroyed that. It hanged and burned him in effigy, while Oliver himself fled.

Another mob took similar action in Annapolis, but among the other colonies the example of Boston was enough. Collectors refused or resigned their commissions, and many of them were forced to flee or remain on the ships that had brought them from England. The British government was helpless. An act of Parliament simply could not be enforced against colonists who were unwilling to obey. Americans had often evaded the law as laid down in London, slipping by customs officers with smuggled molasses, manufacturing forbidden hats or ironware, or carrying on illegal trade with French and Spanish colonies. But never before had they united to defy Parliament's authority to pass a law.

The American argument was put by a lank back-country lawyer in a fiery speech before the House of Burgesses of Virginia. No one knows exactly what Patrick Henry said, though a generation later it was recalled that he cried something like: "Caesar had his Brutus; Charles I his Cromwell; and George III . . . may profit by their example!" Whatever his words, the Speaker accused him of treason and the Burgesses adopted his resolutions, which stated forcefully the right of Virginians to be taxed only by their own Assembly. The House also declared that Virginians were under no obligation to pay the Stamp Tax and that anyone who upheld it was an enemy of the colony. This was revolutionary defiance. The resolutions circulated among the other colonies, and most joined in similar declarations.

In October, shortly before the tax was to take effect, representatives of nine colonies met in a Stamp Act Congress in New York and in the strongest terms declared the Stamp Act unconstitutional. The Congress made no recommendations for action, but none was necessary. The colonists already had taken matters into their own hands. Not only had Stamp Tax collectors been driven from office, but ship captains had been forced to sail, newspapers to publish, taverns to open, and courts to sit without stamped paper. And British products were boycotted by associations of merchants in the port cities.

Faced with the impossibility of collecting the tax and with pressure from British merchants whose trade was suffering, Parliament reluctantly re-

pealed the Stamp Act—but not without passing a Declaratory Act asserting Parliament's unlimited authority to legislate for the colonies. Parliament thought the combination of repeal and the Declaratory Act would show that the government was generous but firm. Americans thought it evidence that the ministry was hostile, but weak and easily intimidated.

Two years later Britain tried again. Aware that the colonies had never denied Parliament's right to regulate trade, even when tariff duties were one of the means of regulation, young Charles Townshend, the new Chancellor of the Exchequer, assumed that they would object only to "internal" taxes collected within the colonies. Ingeniously, he applied "external" taxes on the colonies' imports of paint, lead, glass, paper, and tea. He expected them to be accepted without protest.

Indeed, the response was less clear-cut than that to the Stamp Tax. It was not until John Dickinson, a keen, conservative Philadelphia lawyer, aroused the colonists that they fully understood the issue. Dickinson wrote a series of *Letters from a Farmer in Pennsylvania to the Inhabitants of the British Colonies* which became an immediate best-seller throughout America. Dickinson exploded the distinction between internal and external taxes, and made it clear that the difference was really between measures to regulate trade and measures to raise a revenue. Parliament obviously would not lay duties to discourage the purchase of British goods by Americans, and the Townshend duties had specifically been declared by Parliament to be for the purpose of raising a revenue. After the publication of Dickinson's *Letters* the assemblies of one colony after another—in Massachusetts first of all—passed resolutions opposing the Townshend duties as unconstitutional. They were dissolved immediately by the royal governors.

More effective than protests was another boycott of taxed items in particular and British products generally. Associations to refrain from im-

Opening pages: Notorious Stamp Act of 1765 required
embossed revenue stamps on American documents, here a bill
of lading of a Boston brig bound for Gibralter.
A storm of protest blew up. Americans regarded stamps as taxation
without representation and a threat to self-rule.

porting British goods were organized by merchants of the port cities as in 1765. But now the colonists took a further step of great importance. When the governor of Virginia dissolved the House of Burgesses in 1769 for having adopted resolutions opposing the Townshend duties, the members simply reconvened as an extralegal body and proclaimed a boycott to be enforced by county committees. This was a truly revolutionary act. It was not simply a protest against British authority, but the establishment of a new authority outside the existing law to exercise powers of government.

Once again nonimportation worked. British merchants joined Americans in petitioning for repeal of the Townshend Acts. The new Prime Minister, Frederick, Lord North, finally led a reluctant Parliament in 1770 to repeal all duties save that on tea. The tax on tea served only a symbolic purpose, as the colonists could easily smuggle what tea they needed from Holland or elsewhere. Americans responded by abandoning nonimportation on everything but tea.

Disagreements between the mother country and the colonies now dwindled to a sullen truce broken by sporadic episodes of violence. British troops had been stationed in key colonial ports. Though they were held under tight discipline there were inevitable clashes with gangs of colonists. In January, 1770, there was a pitched battle between New York gangs and redcoats at Golden Hill, though no one was killed. A smaller brawl in Boston resulted in the deaths of five colonists and was inflated by American propaganda as the Boston Massacre.

Nevertheless, the uneasy tension might have lasted indefinitely if North had not decided on one more attempt to raise a colonial revenue. His primary purpose was to rescue the nearly bankrupt British East India Company in whose warehouses were enormous quantities of tea, unsold in part because of the American boycott. Parliament now provided that all duty levied on tea brought into England would be rebated when it was exported to America. This would make legal tea cheaper than smuggled tea. Moreover, the East India Company was authorized to sell tea through its own agents in America, thus bypassing American importers who were boycotting taxed tea. North hoped that these measures would enable the Company to sell its surplus stock and tempt the Americans to accept parliamentary duties.

Since no new duty was being levied, and since the legislation made tea cheaper, not more expensive, North's scheme was not unreasonable. A few years earlier it probably would have worked. But the preceding eight years of dispute had left Americans both suspicious and well organized. Groups calling themselves Sons of Liberty had come into being, ready to act with petitions, processions, riots, or violence, as the occasion might require. Committees of Correspondence kept the radical groups in touch with one another.

Americans were now prepared and the reaction to the Tea Act was immediate. In every colony local committees backed by threats of force prevented the selling and even, in most instances, the landing of British tea. Only in Massachusetts, where the agents of the East India Company were sons of the royal governor, were the demands of the Sons of Liberty refused. Governor Thomas Hutchinson (a descendant of the religious pioneer Anne) insisted that the tea be landed and the duty paid. The colonists' response was blunt. After a mass meeting in Old South Church shortly before Christmas, 1773, hundreds of men thinly disguised as Mohawk Indians silently boarded the ships, and emptied into the harbor three hundred and forty-two cases of valuable tea.

Britain was outraged. Parliament swiftly passed a series of acts aimed primarily at punishing Massachusetts. In March came the Boston Port Act, closing the port to trade until the destroyed tea was paid for—an extreme penalty, since Boston lived by its trade. In May the Massachusetts Government Act abrogated the colony's charter. Another large body of British regulars was sent to Boston and their commander, General Thomas Gage, was made governor, in effect putting Massachusetts under military rule.

Lord North and Parliament gambled that responsible leaders of the other colonies would recoil from the deliberate destructiveness of the Boston Tea Party. They hoped the British response would be seen as proper punishment for the lawless and rebellious citizens of Massachusetts alone. A decade before that might have been the case; many colonial leaders did deplore the Tea Party as reckless and unjustified. But they realized that if Parliament could act as it had with Massachusetts, it could change any of their governments as it willed, disregard their charters, take their leaders to England for trial, and force a standing army on them to suppress all opposition. The colonies moved promptly not only to meet the British threat, but to meet it jointly. Far from abandoning Massachusetts, they called for a Continental Congress to meet at Philadelphia in September, 1774.

Fifty-six delegates sent by twelve of the thirteen colonies (only Georgia was unrepresented) convened at Carpenters' Hall in answer to the call. They were a remarkable group of men. The brace of Adamses (John and Samuel) from Massachusetts, Silas Deane, John Jay, William Livingston, Thomas Mifflin, John Dickinson, Caesar Rodney, John Rutledge, and Christopher Gadsden were among them. The Virginia delegation was particularly distinguished, including Richard Bland, Benjamin Harrison, Patrick Henry, Richard Henry Lee, Peyton Randolph, and George Washington.

Nine of the fifty-six had been members of the Stamp Act Congress in 1765. All of them were leaders of a movement born in that controversy and shaped and hardened in the bitter years that followed. They did not, in fact, think of themselves as radicals or revolutionaries, but as men seeking to recover and preserve a liberty of which they thought themselves the rightful heirs. They were men who ruled themselves and their commonwealths and would yield that rule to no one.

The delegates could readily agree on the definition of colonial rights. But were these enjoyed because they were Englishmen entitled to traditional English rights? Or was the proper ground of protest that the colonies, though parts of the king's domain, were not parts of Great Britain and hence under their charters subject only to the legislation of their own assemblies, rather than that of the British Parliament? Or were the rights they defended theirs because they were the rights of all men? These were inconsistent theories and the difference between them was important. The first could be a basis only of protest and petition, the second of resistance to Parliament within the empire ruled by the Crown. Only the last, which did not rest on English law or colonial charters, could be used as the justification for independence. However inconsistently, Congress resolved the debate by using all three arguments: " . . . the inhabitants of the English colonies in North America, by the immutable laws of nature, the principles of the English constitution, and the several charters or compacts, have the following rights. . . ."

The other great question was what action to take. There was little the Congress could do in fact. A petition to the king was drawn up, offering the colonists' views in loyal and respectful, even affectionate, terms. It was accompanied by an address to the British people, appealing eloquently to English traditions of liberty. And it was accompanied also by measures banning all trade with Great Britain.

The more radical members of Congress had no expectation that the petition or address would be heeded. But they knew that they could not unite the colonies more vigorously until every effort at reconciliation had been exhausted. Having done all it could for the moment, Congress adjourned.

*Defiance: In hall of the House of Burgesses at Williamsburg
(below), Virginia assembly led by Patrick Henry declared it had
"the only and sole exclusive right and power to lay
taxes . . . upon the inhabitants of this Colony." Colonists
united behind their rebellious leaders. Sam Adams and James Otis
held protest meetings in Boston's Faneuil Hall
(opposite). A Stamp Act Congress convened in New York.
A boycott of British goods hastened repeal of the Act (noted on
teapot, far right), but other repressive taxes followed.
British troops were garrisoned in America, clashed
with patriots in 1771, resulting in so-called Boston Massacre
(illustrated in Paul Revere's inflammatory print, top).*

189

Boston Tea Party, conceived by radical Sam Adams and carried out by colonists disguised as Indians, started from Old South Church (opposite) and dumped tea into harbor from chests like that at top left. While outrageous acts fueled the flames of rebellion, leaders like George Mason gave philosophical substance to the cause. Seated at his desk (above), he wrote Virginia Declaration of Rights, asserting "That all men are by nature equally free and independent." In Philadelphia, fifty-five representatives from twelve colonies met at Carpenters' Hall (l) in First Continental Congress to search for a united course of action. Even at this point, delegates were hopeful of reconciliation with the mother country.

THE
PROCEEDINGS
OF THE
VIRGINIA
CONVENTION
IN THE TOWN OF
RICHMOND
ON THE 23ᵈ OF MARCH
1775

*"Is life so dear or peace so sweet as to be
purchased at the price of chains and slavery? Forbid it,
Almighty God! I know not what course others may take,
but as for me, give me liberty or give me death!"
With these words to the Virginia Convention at St. John's
Church in Richmond (opposite & above), Patrick Henry
expressed the growing militancy of America. Throughout
the colonies, extralegal governments had evolved
from elected assemblies that had been dissolved by royal
governors but refused to adjourn. Minutemen were recruited,
military stores gathered, and close watch kept on the
British by Committees of Correspondence. Sons of Liberty,
with symbolic caps (above r), fired patriot hearts.*

10.
The
Revolution

When the Continental Congress reconvened in May, 1775, the Revolution had begun. The king had refused to consider the colonists' petition; the House of Lords had spurned William Pitt's last noble effort at reconciliation; the House of Commons with equal force had quashed similar proposals offered by Edmund Burke and supported by his magnificent address, "On Conciliation with America." Royal governors had been instructed to dissolve colonial assemblies that adopted or considered measures in support of the protest movement. As a result, in most of the colonies no lawful legislature was in being and the actual conduct of government had passed into the hands of provincial congresses, Committees of Safety, and other bodies not recognizing royal authority. Throughout the colonies the popular leaders were in control. Only by the acquiescence of almost helpless Crown officials was violence avoided.

The period of uneasy peace ended in April. London had been pressing General Gage to make more active use of the regiments stationed in Boston to suppress disloyal local authorities. After long hesitation he sent a large body of troops toward Concord, hoping to capture some of the rebel leaders and a supply of powder and arms. Skirmishes with militia on the Lexington village green and at a bridge at Concord shook the British regulars, and they had to retreat some twenty miles to Boston. Over the long and exhausting march they were harassed and ambushed from every tree and fence until they staggered into their own lines with half their number killed or wounded. Five months earlier George III had written Lord North: " . . . blows must decide whether they are to be subject to this country or independent." The blows now had begun.

The Continental Congress responded immediately. The thousands of New England militiamen who had surrounded Boston after the April bat-tles were taken into the Continental service. George Washington was commissioned a general and sent to Cambridge, Massachusetts, to take command in the name of the Congress. Every colony was advised to set up a government independent of British authority. The Congress issued its own money and took over the Indian and postal services previously handled by royal officials. By the summer of 1775, however weak and loosely organized, an American national government existed, with an army, a treasury, a legislature, and the beginnings of a civil service. London, recognizing that royal authority had been usurped, proclaimed the colonies in a state of rebellion.

This was essentially a declaration of war, and intermittent conflict filled the year following Lexington and Concord. A few dozens of irregular American troops captured the old British fort at Ticonderoga, controlling the route from Montreal to New York. Over the winter of 1775–76 a dual attack was made on Canada. Benedict Arnold led one band of Americans through the frozen forests of Maine to threaten Quebec. Richard Montgomery led another small expedition up the Lake Champlain route against Montreal. Montgomery was killed as Montreal fell, but Quebec stood firm against the combined assault of his men and Arnold's.

The British meanwhile drove the New England militia from Breed's and Bunker hills, overlooking the fortifications of Boston. Raids by British naval forces here and there along the coast did more to anger than to injure the colonials.

The first turning point came after the Americans, in an agony of effort, hauled the heavy guns of Ticonderoga on massive ox-drawn sleds over the Berkshire Mountains and the snow-filled roads of Massachusetts and emplaced them on Dorchester Heights overlooking Boston. Gage's occupation of the city was already useless; it now became untenable. In March, 1775, he abandoned Boston.

With Gage's departure, no meaningful

British authority was left in the colonies. The Americans had drifted into an unsought independence. But ahead lay an ominous war against the world's greatest military power, which only a decade before had defeated the combined empires of Spain and France. The Americans had to prepare to fight this war and to define the ends for which they fought. If they lost, it would be Parliament and the king who would decide their future status. But if the Americans won, what ends should they seek in negotiating?

It was no easy question. On the one hand was the old pride and loyalty, the love of English liberty, fealty to the English Crown, the sense of being part of that band of brothers, the free and Protestant Englishmen who had broken the power of the Catholic empires and conquered half the world. There was the awe of British military and naval power. And there were men of wealth and station who feared that riotous mobs, worthless money, and lower-class pretensions would take over without the stable laws of Britain.

But now a third or more of the Americans were Scots, Scotch-Irish, and Germans, who had little love for England. And the English stock itself was generations away from a dimly recalled homeland. The London government's unheeding hostility, the assaults of British troops, and the hiring of Hessian mercenaries to make war on British subjects all eroded the old loyalty.

A pamphlet did more than any other single force to bring Americans finally to their decision: Thomas Paine's *Common Sense*, published in January, 1776. Paine was no lawyer, no reader of Blackstone and Coke. As a newcomer to America he was not caught in the hackneyed terms of the long debate between colonial assemblies and royal governors, or the distinction between duties to regulate trade and duties to raise revenue. Instead, he saw what seemed to him the simple common sense of the matter with an open and sunlit clarity.

Independence was inevitable. To America, the corrupt and selfish rule of a distant British king was a burden without benefits. There was in any case a war to fight and win. It would be better fought and easier won if all joined for independence; and once the war was won it would be unthinkable to throw away the hard-earned gains. Paine brought eloquence to his argument and a perception that American freedom could have meaning for the whole world: "The sun never shined on a cause of greater worth. 'Tis not the affair of a city, a county, a province, or a kingdom, but of a continent. . . . 'Tis not the concern of a day, a year, or an age; posterity are virtually involved in the contest, and will be more or less affected, even to the end of time, by the proceedings now."

One hundred and twenty thousand copies of Paine's pamphlet were sold within three months—one for every four or five families in the colonies. Probably most literate Americans had read it by the spring of 1776. Paine's words crystallized the ideas forming in their minds. The New England colonies were ready for independence, but waited for southern leadership in order to make it a truly continental movement. In April, the North Carolina Provincial Congress took the lead by instructing its delegates to the Continental Congress to vote for independence. In June, Richard Henry Lee of Virginia rose to move the Continental Congress that "these united colonies are, and of right ought to be, free and independent states."

A vote on Lee's resolution was delayed while efforts were pressed to get unanimous support. Many delegates lacked recent instructions from their provinces, and the middle colonies in particular were hesitant. But when the vote came in July, only the New York delegation, bound by old instructions, could not support Lee's motion. In order not to cast a negative vote, it abstained, and independence was voted, 12-0.

Opening pages: Flintlock musket fires a shot heard 'round the world. "We fight," wrote Thomas Paine, touching the heart of the feeling for independence in The American Crisis, *"not to enslave, but to set a country free, and to make room upon the earth for honest men to live in."*

Anticipating the vote, Congress had set up a committee chaired by Thomas Jefferson, with John Adams, Benjamin Franklin, Robert Livingston, and Roger Sherman as members, to draft a formal declaration of independence. Jefferson did most of the drafting, with some help from Adams and Franklin. The completed document was ready for Congress in late June, but was not taken up until independence was actually voted. Congress made a number of amendments, in particular eliminating Jefferson's vigorous attack on slavery, but finally approved the amended document unanimously on July 4.

Most of the Declaration was devoted to a recital of the evil acts of George III. It was poor history but useful propaganda. For years the colonial leaders had declared their loyalty to the king and their faith in his good will, while protesting acts of Parliament. Now they had to persuade Americans to throw off their last loyalty, to the Crown itself, and to achieve this it was politic to attribute to the king a policy of consistent hostility toward the colonies.

But the essence of the Declaration was in its first paragraph. The ideas there set forth were not new, nor was novelty its purpose. The intent was to state to a candid world the beliefs Americans already held. This it did with timeless clarity. Since the Americans were abandoning their charters and seceding from the Empire, they could no longer plead charter rights or the rights of Englishmen. They had to base their Declaration on rights common to all men, everywhere, and always:

"We hold these truths to be self-evident, that all men are created equal, that they are endowed by their Creator with certain unalienable rights, that among these are life, liberty, and the pursuit of happiness. That to secure these rights, governments are instituted among men, deriving their just powers from the consent of the governed, that whenever any form of government becomes destructive of these ends, it is the right of the people to alter or abolish it, and to institute new government, laying its foundations on such principles and organizing its powers in such form, as to them shall seem most likely to effect their safety and happiness."

The deed was done. The independence that was declared already existed in fact. From New Hampshire to Georgia there was no spot left where the king's authority was recognized, or his commands could be enforced. The war that lay ahead would not be an effort of the Americans to throw off British rule, but of the British to invade and conquer the new nation.

That invasion was about to begin. As the delegations to the Continental Congress one by one gave their solemn assent to the Declaration of Independence, British warships and transports lay off Staten Island in New York harbor. They were under the command of Admiral Sir Robert Howe, and the troops aboard were commanded by his brother, General William Howe. The Howes came with an offer of amnesty, pardon, and a discussion of grievances if the Americans would return to their loyalty, and with arms for their conquest if they would not.

No meaningful discussions with the American authorities proved possible. After some weeks of peaceful occupation of Staten Island, General Howe reluctantly moved his troops, without opposition, across the Narrows to Long Island. Thus began more than five years of war.

Patriotic recollection has seen the conflict as one between the American David and the British Goliath, in which only heroic courage, steadfast devotion, military skill, and divine Providence enabled the handful of colonials to defeat the vast might of the British Empire. In fact it was the other way about. Unless the Americans abandoned their cause, the British undertaking was hopeless. They were trying to invade and conquer a nation of more than three million people, stretched over a coastline of eighteen hundred miles and reaching two hundred miles into a nearly roadless interior. And they were to do this with an army transported and supplied over more than three thousand miles of ocean in small, slow sailing vessels. It had taken the British and Americans together seven years to defeat fifty thousand French in Canada. To suppose that without colonial help the British could ever conquer sixty times as many Americans spread over a far larger area of settlement was fantasy.

At least it was fantasy as long as Americans could hold to their cause. It would not be necessary for them to defeat British armies in the field, but it would be necessary for them to endure. For year after long year they would have to keep faith through defeat, through adversity, poverty, and failure, until the British ultimately would be forced to recognize the hopelessness of their attempt to subdue a free people.

The British could maintain an army capable of defeating any force brought against it. They could seize and hold any city, indeed, any two cities, they wished on the American coast. But they could not sustain themselves away from a source of supply. No detachment was safe away from its base; troops could not assert British authority beyond the range of their guns. The amorphous and unorganized character of the new American nation was part of the British problem. There was no capital or center of industry whose conquest would overthrow the whole. One who captured Paris defeated France; if London fell the Empire would fall. But the British could seize Boston or New York or Philadelphia or Charleston without serious effect on the American cause.

Whatever hope of success the British had was based on self-delusion about the strength of Loyalist sentiment in America. It probably was true that only a minority of Americans was actively and zealously seeking independence. But most of the remainder were indifferent rather than devoted to the Crown. American patriots were not desperate revolutionists seeking to overthrow existing authority. For the most part they *were* the local authorities, resisting British efforts to establish what they considered an alien control. They were ruthless in suppressing Tory Loyalists, not hesitating to confiscate estates, destroy businesses, decree imprisonment. It took a bold man to express openly his devotion to the Crown. Everywhere the British were disappointed in their hopes for Loyalist uprisings.

In the summer of 1776, however, their confidence was undimmed, and General Howe moved in a leisurely and professional fashion to capture New York and make it the base of his operations. The island city could not be defended against a superior army with naval support in command of the surrounding waters. The only sensible course would have been to burn it and abandon the site, but the American authorities were not ready to commit so ruthless an act. Instead, Washington marched his untrained army down from Boston and attempted a feckless defense, rashly dividing his forces between Manhattan and Long Island. He was soundly beaten on Brooklyn Heights, and only by luck was able to extricate the troops back to Manhattan. Rashly again he kept his men concentrated at the foot of the island. He escaped being trapped by a British landing in mid-Manhattan only by beating a hasty retreat up the west side of the island to Harlem. The campaign of 1776 ended with the British forces firmly in control of New York City and its environs and of northern New Jersey to the Delaware River. Washington, having retreated to the Delaware's bank to protect Philadelphia, broke the string of American defeats with a daring raid across the icy river to smash the Hessians at Trenton and Princeton. These victories, however, had more psychological than military significance.

The British plan for the second year of the war was to gain control of the Lake Champlain-Hudson River line, to cut off the rebellious New England colonies and capture the American capital at

Philadelphia. An army was launched southward from Canada under the command of General John Burgoyne. That dapper officer probably expected a British army to move up the Hudson to meet him, but Howe instead moved on Philadelphia, leaving General Sir Henry Clinton with a relatively small garrison in New York. He reasoned that this would occupy the Americans as fully as a march up the Hudson, thus preventing Washington from sending troops against Burgoyne, and would yield more rewarding results. Howe did not attempt a crossing of the Delaware in the face of Washington's army, but moved his forces by sea to the head of Chesapeake Bay and marched overland. In spite of a hard-fought battle at Brandywine Creek, Washington was unable to hold the city. The Congress fled to York, Washington took up quarters at Valley Forge, and the war went on.

Meanwhile, Burgoyne was in trouble. The northern wilderness and the long distances over which his troops had to be supplied were his principal enemies. But he was also constantly nibbled at by local militia. Finally, with his supplies and men exhausted he was defeated at Saratoga by a force of Continentals and militia under the command of Horatio Gates and Benedict Arnold. He was forced to surrender with his entire army.

Saratoga was a stunning victory for the Americans, but most importantly it encouraged France to recognize and enter into an alliance with the new nation. The Treaty of Alliance with France was signed in early 1778, a triumph of Benjamin Franklin's diplomacy at Versailles. Undercover French aid had already been helpful. Now aid would be open and generous, and would affect decisively the remaining years of the war.

Realizing that the capture of Philadelphia had done nothing to break American resistance, the British decided to abandon it and unite their forces once more in New York. Withdrawing across New Jersey in June, the British were subjected to a slashing American attack which failed only because of the confusion or disobedience of General Charles Lee, another former British regular with an inflated reputation. It was Washington's last battle until the war's end, more than three years away.

The British now entertained little hope of reconquering America as a whole but they still believed they could detach the weaker southern colonies, where Loyalist sentiment was thought to run high. In December a British fleet and small expeditionary force captured Savannah and with it control over thinly populated Georgia. Seventeen seventy-nine was a year of regrouping and of struggles on other fronts with France, now joined by Spain. But in 1780 the conquest of the South was seriously undertaken. Charleston was attacked by sea and captured, along with a large force of Continentals under General Benjamin Lincoln. British forces under General Charles Cornwallis moved inland, defeated the Americans under Gates at Camden, South Carolina, and by the end of the year controlled most of the state and had penetrated North Carolina.

Nathanael Greene, Washington's favorite general, was put in command of the American forces in the South after Lincoln's capture and Gates' defeat. His army was large enough to threaten Cornwallis and prevent him from utilizing small units to control the countryside. Greene retreated before Cornwallis, drawing him farther and farther from his sources of supply, until he could turn on the British at Guilford Courthouse, North Carolina. Here a major battle was fought in 1781. It ended indecisively, but it cost Cornwallis irreplaceable men and supplies.

Cornwallis's position had become untenable. Local militia in the Carolinas harassed his forces, successfully engaging British detachments in skirmishes and minor battles like those at King's Mountain and Cowpens. Patriot forces had recovered effective control over the countryside in the Carolinas and Georgia. Cornwallis's troops were dwindling. He decided to move north to Virginia and join small British units already operating there, abandoning the colonies to the south except for their major ports.

The combined British forces took Richmond, almost captured Governor Thomas Jefferson at his home near Charlottesville, and then moved to Yorktown, a deep-water port near Williamsburg, on the peninsula between the James and York rivers. Here, it was thought, General Clinton could reinforce and resupply Cornwallis's weary army.

And so it might have happened, but for a stroke of good fortune for the Americans. A French fleet under Admiral de Grasse obtained temporary command of the sea off the Atlantic Coast and was able to control the entrances to New York harbor and to Chesapeake Bay. This was a golden opportunity to use the large, well-equipped, and professionally trained French army under General Rochambeau that had been sent to Washington's aid, and that for more than a year had been lying idle in western Connecticut. Washington was elated and proposed a combined attack on New York. Rochambeau's wiser judgment prevailed. He realized that de Grasse probably could not sustain control of the sea long enough for the slow and uncertain siege against Clinton's main army. Instead, Rochambeau proposed that his and Washington's forces, which were rested and had been well-armed and equipped with French aid, move swiftly south and attack Cornwallis at Yorktown.

Washington reluctantly acquiesced and the complex maneuver was perfectly executed. Cornwallis was trapped. With supplies and ammunition nearly exhausted, and with no hope of early relief, Cornwallis surrendered on October 19, 1781. The British band played "The World Turned Upside Down" as the defeated redcoats stacked their muskets. Yorktown was more a French victory than an American one. De Grasse's fleet made it possible. The plan and most of the regular troops were Rochambeau's. The arms and even the uniforms of the Americans had largely been supplied by France, and French artillery and engineers were the key to the siege. Yet it was Washington to whom Cornwallis surrendered and the American cause that triumphed. For the war was over, though neither side knew it.

II

The Continental Congress, although it had raised an army, created a navy, declared independence, sent ambassadors abroad, and contracted alliances, was not a legal entity. Its authority was only what it assumed and the states were willing to see it exercise. This was obviously an unworkable situation, and as independence approached Congress appointed not only a committee to draft a declaration but also a parallel committee, chaired by John Dickinson, to draw up a frame of government for the new nation.

Dickinson's committee presented a draft of Articles of Confederation that would do little more than formalize the powers already assumed by the Continental Congress. There would be a Congress of the Confederation in which every state had an equal vote. The Congress could raise an army and navy, conduct foreign relations, and carry on war. But it could not regulate trade, or levy taxes, or create law. The states were willing to yield little more power to an American Congress than to a British Parliament. Even this feeble gesture toward central authority was accepted reluctantly. The Continental Congress was slow to pass the Articles and the states slower to ratify them. Not until 1781, five years after they were introduced and just as the war was ending, did they finally come into effect.

The struggle over their ratification, however, gave the Congress of the Confederation the little real authority it was to have. The smaller states, like Maryland, with no claims to western land, refused to ratify until Virginia and other states with enormous western claims agreed to surrender them to the Confederation. Virginia did so, and the lands north of the Ohio, stretching from Pennsylvania to the

Mississippi, came under the sole government of the Congress of the Confederation.

While they fought a war and worked to organize a central government, Americans were re-shaping their society and the constitutions of their individual states. At the moment the Continental Congress was declaring that all men were created equal and endowed with equal rights, the inequalities inherited from Britain persisted. Only landowners could vote and the landless were taxed by assemblies in which they had no more representation than they had in Parliament. Back-country voters were grossly underrepresented in the assemblies of the new states. Dissenters were taxed to support established churches they abhorred. The free land of the early colonial years was all taken up or locked away in the hands of absentee landlords. No longer could a man carve out a freehold by his own hard labor. For most of the poor there remained only the distant frontier, or the tenant's lot working a rich man's land. The class structure was growing more rigid.

The gravest of all inequalities was that suffered by blacks. Four hundred thousand Americans were slaves, bound to unending and unpaid labor. They were not among the men the revolutionists thought of as created equal or as possessed of any rights at all.

Some of these many inequalities the Revolutionary movement began to reduce. Though some property qualification for voting remained everywhere in effect, lower requirements and a broader distribution of property enlarged the franchise. In the Revolutionary years the unequal representation of western counties in the state legislatures was sharply reduced. The Congregational church remained firmly established in New England, but elsewhere church establishment weakened or disappeared.

New states, except Connecticut and Rhode Island, whose liberal colonial charters served well enough, replaced royal governors and appointed councils with elected executives and senates. Bills of rights adopted by the states embodied the principles of the Declaration of Independence and assured the civil liberties of the citizens.

In Massachusetts the state courts held that the bill of rights had abolished slavery. Elsewhere manumission was made easier and the tentative beginnings of an antislavery movement stirred. Several states passed laws forbidding the further importation of slaves. But nothing further was achieved toward racial equality. A few Quakers and troubled clergy were sensitive to the abyss of contradiction between the ideals of the Declaration and the fact of human slavery, but their voices went almost unheard. The silent response to the challenge of "All men are created equal" was not to accept blacks as equal, but to deny they were "men" in the meaning of the Declaration.

The most effective step the Revolutionary generation took to establish equality was to free land. The holdings of the Crown, the great proprietors, and the wealthy Tory landlords were confiscated and passed, mostly as small holdings, into private hands. Public lands were made easily available, and the vast abundance of the West was thrown open to settlement. Free land resumed its role as the great solvent of social classes and economic oppression in American life.

Matching these political and economic measures was an upsurge of popular emotion, an egalitarian air of freedom, an overthrow of old deferences that was to grow steadily until it triumphed in Jacksonian democracy and became the characteristic stamp of the American spirit.

The government under the Articles of Confederation came into formal existence only a few months before the British defeat at Yorktown, too late to have any important effect on the conduct of the war. Its real test came in negotiating the treaty of peace that ended the war. At the moment of Cornwallis's surrender it was by no means clear that the war was over. The British still held New York and Charleston. Their armies remained more powerful than any the Americans could bring against them. The French government was facing financial embarrassment, and probably would not continue its support of the American cause with armies and fleets.

But the British people had had enough. Britain needed peace, not only with the Americans, but with the French and Spanish, who were winning victories in the West Indies, the Mediterranean, and Asia. George III was willing to fight stubbornly on, but his subjects were not. In 1782 Parliament voted that anyone who attempted or advised the continuance of the war in America was an enemy of the country. Lord North's ministry fell, clearing the way to negotiations for peace.

The United States was represented at Paris by John Adams, Benjamin Franklin, and John Jay. The Treaty of Alliance with France obligated each party not to make peace without the other, and France and Spain were not eager to see the United States win too great a diplomatic victory. France would have liked the new nation to be a relatively weak protégé, dependent on her for protection from Great Britain. Spain was especially anxious to keep Americans distant from her trans-Mississippi territories. Vergennes, the skillful and sophisticated French minister of foreign affairs, who was host at the conference, supported American independence, but did his suave best to control negotiations in the interests of France and Spain. On Jay's and Adams's insistence, however, and with Franklin's somewhat troubled concurrence, the American representatives dealt separately and in part secretly with the British and won a diplomatic triumph.

American independence was conceded fully and unconditionally. The Mississippi was defined as the western boundary of the new nation, and Britain recognized American freedom to navigate that stream. The right to fish off Newfoundland was recognized, though only the "liberty," not the right, to land and dry fish on its shores. The British promised early withdrawal from their western outposts. The only object the Americans seriously sought and failed to get was the same trading and commercial rights in the British Empire that they had enjoyed as colonies. The British insisted on reserving discussion of this subject for a later commercial treaty.

In return, the American representatives promised only that no obstacles would be placed in the way of the collection of British debts through the normal processes of law and that the Congress would "recommend" to the states a restoration of Loyalist property, a provision which both sides knew was an empty formality. Their achievement has been called "the greatest victory in the annals of American diplomacy."

Agreement was reached in early November, 1782, and the treaty was signed on November 30. To preserve the American commitment not to make a separate peace, it was provided, however, that it would not come into final effect until the signing of a peace treaty between England and France. It was nearly a year before that occurred, but the American victory was already completed. The colonial era was ended. The new nation had come to be. The independence declared seven long years past was now recognized by all the world. There, sealed with wax, were the words:

"His Britannic Majesty acknowledges the said United States, viz. New Hampshire, Massachusetts Bay, Rhode Island, and Providence Plantations, Connecticut, New York, New Jersey, Pennsylvania, Delaware, Maryland, Virginia, North Carolina, South Carolina, and Georgia, to be free, sovereign and independent States; that he treats with them as such, and for himself, his heirs and successors, relinquishes all claims to the Government, proprietary and territorial rights of the same, and every part thereof."

Like lowering skies swirling about the spire of Boston's Old North Church (l), the Revolution came at last to the American colonies—foreboding, disruptive, and with consequences no man could foretell. Thousands of redcoats controlled Boston. In Concord patriots had laid by arms and munitions. In Lexington, Sam Adams and John Hancock, whose plotting had brought tensions to the breaking point, were staying in the Hancock-Clarke house (below). On the night of April 18, 1775, the British took action.

The Midnight Ride: When the British move was detected, a prearranged signal —"two if by sea"—was flashed from the tower of Old North Church (r & l), and Paul Revere, a courier for the Committee of Correspondence, ran out the rear of his house (below), was rowed across the Charles River under a rising moon, and—by his own account—"got a horse of Deacon Larkin" in Charlestown. Evading a British patrol, he "alarmed almost every house till I got to Lexington."

Lexington: Shortly after midnight the belfry bell rang. Minutemen mustered under Captain John Parker, then repaired to Buckman Tavern (below) to await the redcoats. At dawn the British arrived. Billy Diamond beat his drum (bottom l) and redcoats and rebels faced off across the green. "Disperse, ye rebels, disperse!" ordered Major John Pitcairn. A single shot followed, then volleys of British fire. Right: Musket of mortally wounded Jonathon Harrington, Jr. Hancock and Adams retreated to a nearby barn, were served refreshments in pewter tankards (bottom r).

Concord: By midmorning 400 patriots were challenging the British at North Bridge (below). Three redcoats and two Americans died. The British retreated, regrouped, and turned back toward Boston. At Meriam's Corner fighting erupted again. Minutemen—now 1,000 strong—fought Indian-style from behind trees and stone walls. Major Pitcairn lost his horse (his pistols, l, recovered at Bunker Hill). At Bloody Angle (r) eight redcoats died—and so it was throughout the long retreat to Boston. Casualties: 273 British, 95 Americans. "Blows must decide," King George had said. Blows had now begun.

Congress assumed the reins of government, enrolled the 15,000 militiamen surrounding Boston in a Continental army. George Washington was commissioned a general, stayed a night in the Hopkins House (bottom) at Providence on way to Cambridge to take command. Ethan Allen and his Green Mountain Boys captured Fort Ticonderoga (below) and Crown Point, gaining control of route to Montreal. In June the redcoats took Bunker hill and Breed's hill. Right: Musket was used as club when patriots ran out of ammunition. "A dear-bought victory," wrote British General Clinton. "Another such would have ruined us."

The colonial navy—a few converted merchantmen—was bottled up by the twenty-eight warships, 500 guns, and 4,000 seamen Royal Navy had in America as war began. Opposite & above: Reproduction of HMS Rose, which raided Hudson River and New England coasts. American response was generally limited to opportunistic raids by privateers and to exploits of heroes like John Paul Jones. In Ranger, outfitted at Portsmouth, New Hampshire, shed (l), he raided Britain's home island in 1777-78.

"The sun never shined on a cause of greater worth," wrote Tom Paine in Common Sense, stating the case for independence with passionate conviction and clarity. Below & opposite: An original copy with Paine's writing implements and his table. Desire for a complete and final break with the mother country was far from unanimous, however. Half the population was neutral or pacifist and another ten percent actively Tory. Plaques of King George and Queen Charlotte (r) symbolized traditional English loyalty. Tory military units were enlisted in New York and New Jersey, and in the divided Carolinas there was war between neighbors.

Overleaf: A thousand patriots routed 1,600 Tories at Widow Moore's Creek, North Carolina, in early 1776. More than half the Tory force, mostly backwoods Scots Highlanders marching to rendezvous with a British fleet, were captured. When fleet's attempt to seize Charleston was repulsed four months later, British drive to secure the South was thwarted.

217

Fort Ticonderoga, captured strongpoint on New York-Montreal route, had seige guns (these pages) which Washington needed in Boston. In winter of 1775, patriots loaded them onto ox-drawn sleds and by prodigious effort hauled them 300 miles over snow-covered Berkshire Mountains to Dorchester Heights, overlooking Boston. This strategic advantage made British occupation of the city hopeless, and General Howe withdrew his troops by sea to Halifax, Nova Scotia, to await reinforcements.

Declaration of Independence: Thomas Jefferson's view of proceedings on July 4, 1776, when delegates of thirteen states meeting in council room (r) of Pennsylvania Statehouse in Philadelphia adopted his statement of the American cause— total independence for a new country, with government by consent of the governed. (Jeffersonian walking stick leans against his chair.) Below: Reproduction of travel desk Jefferson used in drafting document. Bottom: Silver inkstand used by delegates signing it.

"*Proclaim Liberty throughout all the Land unto all the Inhabitants thereof*" *was the inscription circling Liberty Bell (opposite) when it rang to celebrate the Declaration of Independence. That event, wrote John Adams, "ought to be solemnized with pomp and parade, with shows, games, sports, guns, bells, bonfires and illuminations from one end of this continent to the other, from this time forward for evermore."*
Right: Independence Hall (Pennsylvania Statehouse), where bell hung in yard. Bottom: Long Room, on second floor, where celebrations took place.

Christmas, 1776: "These are the times that try men's souls," Paine wrote in The Crisis, *as six months of defeat and despair followed the high spirits occasioned by the Declaration. Winter gripped the land, and Washington and his ragged army were camped along the west bank of the Delaware. "The summer soldier and the sunshine patriot will, in this crisis, shrink from the service of his country," Paine cried, "but he that stands it* now, *deserves the love and thanks of man and woman. Tyranny, like hell, is not easily conquered; yet we have this consolation with us, that the harder the conflict, the more glorious the triumph. What we obtain too cheap, we esteem too lightly; 'tis dearness only that gives everything its value. Heaven knows how to put a proper price upon its goods; and it would be strange, indeed, if so celestial an article as* Freedom *should not be highly rated." Opposite & above: Thompson-Neely House, in Bucks County, Pennsylvania, where Christmas-night crossing of Delaware and attack on Trenton were decided.*

Washington Crosses the Delaware: In a desperate move on Christmas
night, Washington took the offensive. Loading a force of some 2,400 men into Durham
boats (r), he crossed the ice-filled river and launched a surprise attack
on the sleeping Hessian garrison at Trenton, capturing nearly 1,000. A week later,
outwitting Cornwallis, he scored another sweet victory at Princeton.
"All our hopes," wrote the British secretary of war, "were blasted by the unhappy
affair at Trenton." Below: Hessian drum, coffee pot, and weapons from Trenton.

1777: Continental Congress resolves "that the flag of the thirteen United States be thirteen stripes, alternate red and white, that the union be thirteen stars, white in a blue field, representing a new constellation." Above: Home of Betsy Ross, widowed Philadelphia seamstress who, traditionally, fashioned the first national emblem. Left: Interior with her thimble and eyeglasses.

Defeat at Brandywine: Washington, seeking to prevent British capture of Philadelphia in 1777, opposed Howe's army at Brandywine Creek (l), near Chadds Ford. Howe's generalship confused and disrupted the Continentals. They lost a hard-fought battle and, ultimately, the city. Washington was repulsed again at Germantown and retreated to Valley Forge. Above, clockwise: Quaker schoolhouse, center of hottest action at Brandywine, changed hands eleven times in forty-five minutes. Headquarters of young Marquis de Lafayette, who made his first appearance here. Birmingham meeting house served as hospital. Washington headquarters.

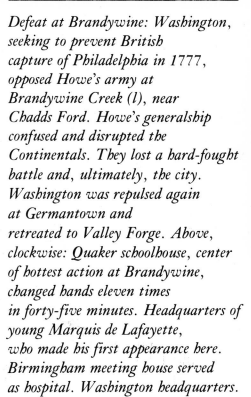

*Victory at Saratoga: "Gentleman Johnny" Burgoyne,
moving south from Montreal in a strategic move to split
New England from the other colonies, exhausted
his men and supplies, and was decisively beaten at
Saratoga, New York, by the American Northern
Army and an aroused countryside.
Burgoyne surrendered to General Horatio Gates with 5,500
men. Above: Freeman's Farm, where patriots led by
Benedict Arnold carried out successful attack. Opposite:
Cards played on gun carriage relieved tedium of
camp life. Right: Knife, musket balls, bullet pouch.*

235

*Saratoga reverberated as far as France. A Treaty of Alliance negotiated
in 1778 by Benjamin Franklin, American commissioner in Paris, assured that French
troops and supplies, backed by the French fleet, would be thrown
into the battle, openly and generously. Opposite: Symbols of French participation
are Lafayette's dress sword and a Charleroi musket with French flag.
Below right: Vernon House at Newport, headquarters of General Rochambeau,
the French commander in America. Below left: Thank-you gift of china to Newport
hostess from wife of French officer quartered in her home.
Overleaf: Valley Forge, Pennsylvania, where Washington and his tattered and
dispirited army spent the bitter winter of 1777-78.*

237

Morristown, 1779-80: In the fifth year of war, the Continental army suffered another bleak New Jersey winter at Jockey Hollow, standing watch on British occupying New York. War in the North was stalemated. In the South it was going badly. Bottom: Reproduction of log-hut encampment built by ill-clothed, half-starved troops. Below: Pile of nearly worthless state-issued banknotes was one man's mustering-out pay. Notes rest on strong boxes of Robert Morris, banker and financial miracle man of Revolution. Left: Washington's office in Ford House. Right: Wick House headquarters of staff general.

240

War in the South: Cornwallis's Carolina Campaign was expected to roll up the rebels. He won at Camden, lost at Cowpens, won expensively at Guilford Courthouse.
Below: At King's Mountain, frontier riflemen destroyed a Loyalist force and killed its commander, Major Ferguson. Left: Cairn of Scotsman Ferguson. Opposite: Spire of St. Michael's Church in Charleston was patriot observation post during British siege of city. Bottom right: "Swamp Fox" Francis Marion, planter and Indian fighter, emerged from boggy hideouts to wage guerrilla war against the British.

*May, 1781: In handsome room of Webb House
at Wethersfield, Connecticut, Washington and
Rochambeau conferred on most effective
use of their combined forces. Washington's ardent
hope was to end war with decisive victory at
New York City, while Rochambeau advanced
more cautious plan for attack on British in the
South. Three months later, when he
learned that Admiral de Grasse would bring his
fleet no farther north than the Chesapeake,
Washington finally acceded to southern campaign
that led to Yorktown, final British defeat.*

Yorktown is the objective! The combined land-sea forces converge on Virginia. De Grasse's control of sea lanes prevents British fleet from aiding Cornwallis. Flags fly, bullets are molded, drums beat a rataplan as noose tightens around British. Overleaf: Redoubt #9 in Allies' forward siege line on battlefield of Yorktown. The complex operation was perfectly executed by French and Americans, and Cornwallis surrendered as a British band played "The World Turned Upside Down."

"The play is over, the fifth act has come to an end," said Lafayette. Right: Surrender room in Moore House, where final terms were drawn. Above: Surrender field where British troops stacked their arms. Field marquee (l) of General Washington, and cave (top) which served Cornwallis as headquarters at end of the siege.

A new nation was born when John Adams pressed his signet ring (r) into the wax on Treaty of Paris in 1782. Top: First official American eagle (in reverse on Great Seal of the United States). Above: First Purple Heart, awarded for bravery. "His Britannic Majesty," said the Treaty, "acknowledges the said United States . . . to be free, sovereign and independent States. . . ."

Credits *In order of appearance.*

Colonial National Park, VA, pages 2-3, 4-5, 10-11, 248-249, 250-251.

Charles Towne Landing, Charleston, SC, pages 6-7, 103.

Cape Cod National Seashore, MA, pages 8-9.

The Jamestown Foundation, Jamestown, VA, pages 16-17, 26-27, 28-29.

Plimoth Plantation, Plymouth, MA, pages 30-31, 32-33, 35, 36-37, 38-39, 140-141.

Pilgrim Hall Museum, Plymouth, MA, pages 32, 34.

Plymouth Antiquarian Society, Plymouth, MA, pages 32, 34, 134-135, 141, 158.

Bennington Museum, Inc., Bennington, VT, pages 40-41, 62.

Town of Sandwich, MA, pages 46, 49.

Ipswich Historical Society, Ipswich, MA, page 47.

Smith's Castle, Wickford, RI, page 48.

Topsfield Historical Society, Topsfield, MA, page 48.

Jenny Grist Mill, Plymouth, MA, page 50.

Saugus Iron Works National Historic Site, Saugus, MA, page 51.

House of Seven Gables Settlement Association, Salem, MA, page 53.

The Society for the Preservation of New England Antiquities, Boston, MA, page 53.

The Old Gaol Museum, York, ME, pages 54, 57, 189.

Society for the Preservation of Historic Landmarks in York County, York, ME, pages 54, 57.

Trinity Church in Newport, Newport, RI, pages 54-55.

Harvard University, Cambridge, MA, page 56.

The Old Ship Meeting House, Hingham, MA, pages 57, 123.

Old Deerfield Heritage Foundation, Deerfield, MA, pages 58-59.

The Essex Institute, Salem, MA, pages 60, 189.

Salem Maritime National Historic Site, Salem, MA, page 61.

Mr. Richard Bole, Shelburne, MA, page 62.

The Preservation Society of Newport County, Newport, RI, page 62.

Mr. John Hetzel, Coventry, CT, pages 62-63.

Pennsylvania Farm Museum, Lancaster, PA, pages 64-65.

Old Merion Meetinghouse, Ardmore, PA, page 70.

The Historical Society of Pennsylvania, Philadelphia, PA, pages 71, 240.

Pennsbury Manor, Tullytown, PA, page 71.

Christ Church, Philadelphia, PA, page 72.

Elfreth's Alley Association, Philadelphia, PA, pages 74-75.

The Franklin Institute, Philadelphia, PA, pages 76-77.

Independence National Historic Park, Philadelphia, PA, pages 78-79, 222-223, 224-225.

Sleepy Hollow Restorations, Inc., Tarrytown, NY, pages 80-81, 82, 142, 147

Historic Fallsington, Fallsington, PA, page 83.

Old Swedes Church, Philadelphia, PA, page 83.

Daniel Boone Homestead, Baumstown, PA, page 84.

Colonial Williamsburg Foundation, Williamsburg, VA, pages 86-87, 106-107, 108-109, 142, 144, 150-151, 152-153, 154-155, 156-157, 159, 164-165, 166-167, 168, 188-189, 194-195, 228, 247.

George Washington Birthplace National Monument, VA, pages 92, 100, 103, 110-111, 143, 148-149.

Boone Hall Plantation, Charleston, SC, pages 93, 104-105.

The Robert E. Lee Memorial Foundation, Inc., Westmoreland County, VA, pages 94-95, 98, 101, 102, 104, 145.

Middleton Place Gardens and Plantation Stableyards, Charleston, SC, pages 96-97.

Monticello, Charlottesville, VA, pages 96, 222.

Westover Plantation, VA, pages 96-97.

Board of Regents of Gunston Hall, National Society of Colonial Dames of America, pages 97, 98-99, 146, 149, 191.

Old Salem Inc., Winston-Salem, NC, page 101.

The Mount Vernon Ladies' Association of the Union, Mount Vernon, VA, pages 104, 110, 112-113, 142, 252.

New York State Historic Trust, Washington's Headquarters, Newburgh, NY, pages 110, 212-213, 228, 236, 252.

Alexandria-Washington Lodge No. 2 A.F. & A.M., Alexandria, VA, page 110.

Augustus Lutheran Church, Trappe, PA, pages 114-115, 127.

Bruton Parish Church, Williamsburg, VA, pages 120-121, 166.

Mr. Ebenezer Gay, Hingham, MA, page 122.

Old Fort Niagara Association, Youngstown, NY, pages 124, 170-171, 176-177, 180-181.

The Society of Friends of Touro Synagogue, Newport, RI, page 125.

Old Third Haven Meeting House, Easton, MD, page 126.

Ephrata Cloister, Ephrata, PA, pages 128-129, 130.

The Moravian Congregation of Bethlehem, PA, page 131.

Fruitlands Museum, Harvard, MA, page 132.

The First Baptist Church in America, Providence, RI, page 133.

Valley Forge State Park Commission, Valley Forge, PA, pages 141, 238-239.

The Kenmore Association, Fredericksburg, VA, page 147.

Gilbert Stuart Memorial, Saunderstown, RI, page 149.

The Tryon Palace Commission, New Bern, NC, pages 160-161, 166-167, 168-169.

The Bostonian Society, Old State House, Boston, MA, pages 165, 182-183, 208.

Fort Ticonderoga, Ticonderoga, NY, pages 176, 212, 220-221.

Fort Ligonier Memorial Foundation, Inc., Fort Ligonier, PA, pages 178-179.

Fort Necessity National Battlefield, PA, pages 178-179.

City of Boston, MA, page 189.

Old South Association, Boston, MA, page 190.

Daughters of the American Revolution, Washington, DC, page 191.

The Carpenters' Company, Philadelphia, PA, page 191.

St. John's Episcopal Church, Richmond, VA, pages 192-193.

Christ Church in Boston, Boston, MA, pages 204-205, 206-207.

Lexington Historical Society, Lexington, MA, pages 205, 208-209, 210.

Paul Revere Memorial Association, Boston, MA, page 206.

Minute Man National Historical Park, MA, pages 210-211.

National Society of Colonial Dames of America of Rhode Island and Providence, Providence, RI, page 212.

Mr. John Millar, Newport, RI, pages 214-215.

Huguenot and Historical Association of New Rochelle, New Rochelle, NY, pages 216-217.

Concord Antiquarian Society, Concord, MA, page 217.

Moores Creek National Military Park, NC, pages 218-219.

Washington Crossing State Park Commission, PA, pages 226-227, 228-229.

Old Barracks Association, Trenton, NJ, page 228.

American Flag and Betsy Ross Memorial, Philadelphia, PA, pages 230-231.

Brandywine State Park, PA, pages 232-233.

Birmingham Meeting, Chadds Ford, PA, page 233.

Saratoga National Historical Park, Saratoga, NY, pages 234-235.

Morristown National Historic Park, Morristown, NJ, pages 240-241.

Kings Mountain National Military Park, SC, pages 242-243.

St. Michael's Church, Charleston, SC, page 243.

National Society of the Colonial Dames of America in the State of Connecticut, Wethersfield, CT, pages 244-245.

The Smithsonian Institution, Washington, DC, page 250.

Adams National Historic Site, Quincy, MA, page 253.

Index

A

Adams, John, 118, 198, 203, 224, *252*
Adams, Samuel, 187, *188, 191, 205*
Agriculture, *93, 103*
Alamance, battle of, 163
Allen, Ethan, *212, 220*
Amadas, Philip, 19
Amherst, Jeffrey, 175
Andros, Edmund, 25
Anglicanism, *54,* 66, 116, 117
Annapolis, 184
Arnold, Benedict, 196, 200, *235*
Articles of Confederation, 201, 202
Augustus Church, *117*

B

Bacon, Nathaniel, 23
Bacon's and Ingram's Proceedings, 4-5
Baptists, 118, *133*
Barlowe, Arthur, 19
Berkeley, William, 23
Beverley, Robert, 6-7
Bills of rights, 202
Bland, Richard, 187
Boone Hall, *93, 105*
Boston, *57, 60, 165, 188, 191, 205, 210, 212;* battle of, 196, *220*
Boston Latin School, 44
Boston Massacre, 186, *188*
Boston Port Act, 186
Boston Tea Party, 187, *191*
Braddock, Gen. Edward, 174, *179*
Bradford, William, *8-9, 30, 35*
Brandywine Creek, battle of, 200, *233*
Breed's hill, battle of, 196, *212*
British East India Company, 186
Bruton Parish Church, *120*
Buckman Tavern, *208*
Bunker Hill, battle of, 196, *212*
Burgoyne, Gen. John, 200, *235*
Burke, Edmund, 196
Byrd, William, *97*

C

Cabot, John, 19
Canada, campaign in, 196
Candles, 138
Cape Cod, *8-9*
Cape Henry, *2-3*
Carpenters' Hall (Philadelphia), *191*
Catholic Church, *125*
Charleston, 90, *97,* 200, *217, 242*

Chesapeake Bay, 201
Christ Church (Philadelphia), *72*
Clinton, Sir Henry, 200, 201, *212*
Clothmaking, 137
Coke, Edward, 44
Colonial governors, 162
Columbus, Christopher, 19
Committees of Correspondence, *193, 206*
Committees of Safety, 196
Common Sense, 197, *217*
Concord, fighting at, 196, *205, 210*
Conestoga wagon, *65*
Congregationalism, 43, 45, 116, *123,* 202
Congress of the Confederation, 201
Connecticut, 25, 45, *59,* 162, 173, 202, *245*
Constitution of the United States, 119
Continental Congress, 187, 196, 197, 201-202, *231*
Cookery, *6-7, 137, 141, 142, 147*
Corn, *38,* 139, *141*
Cornwallis, Gen. Charles, 200, 201, *228, 242, 247, 250*
Cotton, 89
Cotton, John, 43
Cowpens, battle of, *200, 242*
Crafts, 136-139, *151, 153, 157*
Crisis, The, 227
CROATOAN, 20
Crown Point, 174, *176, 212*
Cumberland Gap, 175
Currency, *67,* 196

D

Dale, Thomas, 22
Daniel Boone Homestead, *85*
Dare, Virginia, 20
Deane, Silas, 187
Declaration of Independence, 18, *89,* 119, 197-198, 202, *222*
Delaware, 66
De la Warr, Thomas West, Baron, 22
Derby, Elias Hasket, *60*
Dickinson, John, 185, 187, 201
Discovery, 26
Drake, Sir Francis, 20
Dress, 24, 44, 89, 136, 138
Dunmore, Lord, 175
Dutch Reformed Church, 66, 116

E

East India House, *60*
Education, 43, 45, *57*

Edwards, Jonathan, 117, 118
Emerson-Wilcox House, *54*
Ephrata, *130*

F

Faneuil Hall, 57, *188*
Flag, American, *231*
Foods, 139. *See also* Cookery
Forbes, Gen. John, *179*
Fort Duquesne, 174, 175, *176, 179*
Fort Ligonier, *179*
Fort Necessity, 174, *179*
Fort Niagara, *125, 173,* 175, *176*
Fort Pitt, 175
Fort Ticonderoga, *176,* 196, *212, 220*
France, alliance with colonies, 200; claims, 19, 173-175, *176*
Franklin, Benjamin, 68, 198, 200, 203, *237*
Franklin stove, 77
French and Indian War, *173*
Frontier settlement, 172
Fuller, Samuel, *35*
Furniture, 24, 136
Fur trade, 173, *173*

G

Gadsden, Christopher, 187
Gage, Gen. Thomas, 187, 196, *220*
Gallows Hill, *53*
Gates, Gen. Horatio, 200, *235*
Gates, Sir Thomas, 22
Gay, Ebenezer, *123*
George III, 184, 196, 198, 203, *217*
Georgia, 91, 200
Glassmaking, 137
Godspeed, 26
Gooch, William, *167*
Governor's Council(s), 162
Great Awakening, 118, 119
Great Lakes, 173
Grasse, Admiral de, 201, *245, 247*
Greene, Nathanael, 200
Green Mountain Boys, *212, 235*
Grenville, Sir Richard, 20, 184
Guilford Court house, battle of, 200, *242*
Gunston Hall, *97, 99, 147*

H

Hamilton, Alexander, 69
Hampton plantation, *93*
Hancock-Clarke House, *205*
Hancock, John, *57, 205*
Hariot, Thomas, 20

Harrison, Benjamin, 187
Harrison, Peter, 116
Harvard College, 43, *57*
Henry, Patrick, 116, 163, 185, 187, *188, 191*
Holme, Thomas, 72
Hopkins House, *212*
House of Burgesses, 186, *188*
House of Seven Gables, *53*
Housing, 29, 47, 48, *59,* 138
Howe, Admiral Sir Robert, 198
Howe, Gen. William, 198, 199, 200, *233*
Hoxie House, *47, 48*
Hudson River Valley, *81*
Huguenots, 66, 90, 139
Hutchinson, Anne, 43
Hutchinson, Thomas, 186

I

Indentured servants, 88, 138
Independence Hall, 78, *224*
Indians, 20, 24, 43, 44, 68, 69, 90, 173, 174, 175; wars, 23, 25
Indigo, 90
Industry, 42
Iron industry, *51,* 137

J

Jacksonian democracy, 202
James River, 88
Jamestown, *2-3, 4-5, 10-11,* 18, 19, 20, 21-22, 23, *25, 26,* 29
James II, 25
Jay, John, 187, 203
Jefferson, Thomas, 91, 97, 163, 198, 201, *222*
Jenny, John, 51
Johnson, William, *173,* 174, 175, *180*
Jones, John Paul, *215*
Judaism, 116, *125*
Junto Club, 77

K

Kenmore plantation, *147*
King Philip's War, 25
King's Mountain, battle of, 200, *242*

L

Lafayette, Marquis de, *233, 237, 250*
Lake Champlain, 174, *176*
Lake George, 174
Land distribution, 202
Land speculation, 173
Lane, Ralph, 20

255